HUNT THE FAR MOUNTAIN

ALSO BY KEITH SEVERINSEN
Hunter Climb High

HUNT THE FAR MOUNTAIN

Keith Severinsen

A.H. & A.W. REED WELLINGTON AUCKLAND SYDNEY MELBOURNE

First published 1970
Reprinted 1970

A. H. & A. W. REED LTD
182 Wakefield Street, Wellington
29 Dacre Street, Auckland
51 Whiting Street, Artarmon, Sydney
357 Little Collins Street, Melbourne

© 1970 Keith Severinsen
ISBN 0 589 00422 0

Registered in Australia for transmission by post as a book
Set in 10/12 point Linotype Janson and
Printed in Australia by Halstead Press, Sydney

CONTENTS

PART ONE: SOUTH ISLAND SAFARI
1. Hunters of the Havelock   11
2. Chamois on the High Peaks   17
3. Wallabies of Waimate   23
4. Fallow Deer of Mt Creighton   26
5. Boar at Bay   31

PART TWO: HUNTING THE NORTH ISLAND
6. The Rusa Roared Twice   39
7. Search for a Sika Stag   52
8. Deer of the Kawekas   64
9. Sheep Hunt in Shangri-la   69
10. New Zealand's Toughest Trophy   73
11. On the Trail of a Samba Stag   77

PART THREE: SOUTHLAND AND STEWART ISLAND
12. The Mountains of Mavora   85
13. The One That Got Away!   96
14. The Case of the Crooked Rifle   100
15. The Stags of Mt Aspiring   105
16. South to Stalk Stewart Island   110
17. The Hunters of Half Moon   117

PART FOUR: THE BIG STAGS OF FIORDLAND
18. Call of the Canyon   121
19. West to the Whitewater River   143
20. Food for the Long Trail   159
21. The Mightiest Stag in Fiordland   166
22. The Trail to Never Never   176

LIST OF ILLUSTRATIONS

facing page

American hunter W. Koller looks down the Forbes Valley, across the Havelock to the distant Cloudy Peak Range in South Canterbury	32
Bill Koller with his fourteen-point stag shot in the Forbes	32
A bull thar shot in South Canterbury by American Bill Koller	33
This wallaby from the Hunter Hills fell to rifleman W. Koller	33
A sixteen-point fallow buck shot high on Mt Creighton near Lake Wakatipu	48
On the Trail to Never Never. Wilby at a fly camp in the Harrison River, Fiordland	48
A billy goat trophy taken by W. Koller. Beyond Lake Wakatipu can be seen the valleys of the Greenstone and Caples	49
This huge wild boar was shot on Mararoa Station in Southland	49
A wild boar at bay, surrounded by excited dogs	64
The men of Mararoa Station rope the wild boar	64
Victim of the storm. Lloyd Tillett inspects the half-buried remains of a rusa stag	65
Rusa stags are exceedingly wary, but two were shot in one day	65
Lloyd Tillett with a sika stag	80
The lovely beeches of State Forest 90, south-east of Taupo	80
Two safari groups cross trails	81
An outstanding rusa trophy shot by the author	81
This old shelter in the Mararoa bush is known as "Igly"	112
A tiny shanty lies hidden far up the Whitestone	112

LIST OF ILLUSTRATIONS

facing page

A camp on Kitchener clearing up the east Matukituki	113
A fine buck chamois shot on the slopes of Mt Aspiring	113
Stalker Russell Sattrup looks across to Mt Aspiring, the peak on the right	128
High up on the saddle between Mill Creek and the East Branch of the Matukituki lies a handsome trophy	128
Doug Johnston stows his gear aboard Jimmie Ballantyne's dinghy	129
The Fearful Crags and Canyons of Fiordland. Author with the great sixteen-pointer, high above the canyon of the Light River	129
A fine old whitetail buck	144
Wilby Oliver takes his trophy for a ride in the tractor tube dinghy	144
Wilby Oliver with his Saddle Hill trophy	145
A dead kiwi found high on the snowgrass ridge above George Sound	145
Wilby Oliver gazes down the Stillwater Valley	160
The Mightiest Stag in Fiordland. This outstanding sixteen-pointer red stag is a joint trophy as both stalkers fired simultaneously	160
Joe's River deluge. Cascading waterfalls swell the flooded river during a storm	161
A hidden pool, called Welcome Lake, high in the Fiordland forests	161

The illustrations are from the author's collection.

PREFACE

Today the wild animals of New Zealand are harried as never before. Helicopter gunships slaughter them from the air and venison hunters patrol by day and with spotlights by night. The result is that deer and other wild animals, more wary than ever, have retreated to the remotest regions.

Securing trophies by spotlight is unsporting as far as I am concerned, and I find myself shooting game at much greater distances now than when I first started hunting. The long-range marksmanship described in the following pages is thus an aspect of present-day stalking, aided by extremely accurate rifles and precision telescopic sights.

Venison hunting does not interest me, though I would much rather see a youngster drag a deer carcass from the bush than wastefully let it rot. A trophy hunter does not stalk just to kill animals; he loves, protects, and conserves the dwindling game herds and seldom fires a shot. He searches endlessly for that dream trophy, that magnificent rack of antlers from an outstanding stag.

Many stalkers hunt for a lifetime and never take a winning trophy. But that does not matter; it is the quest that counts, the stalking the sombre bush and climbing the snowgrass heights.

It is the great mates that you make, the endurance, the discomfort, the danger and the vivid memories which put the intangible value into a great game trophy. There is always another valley to explore, and another range ahead.

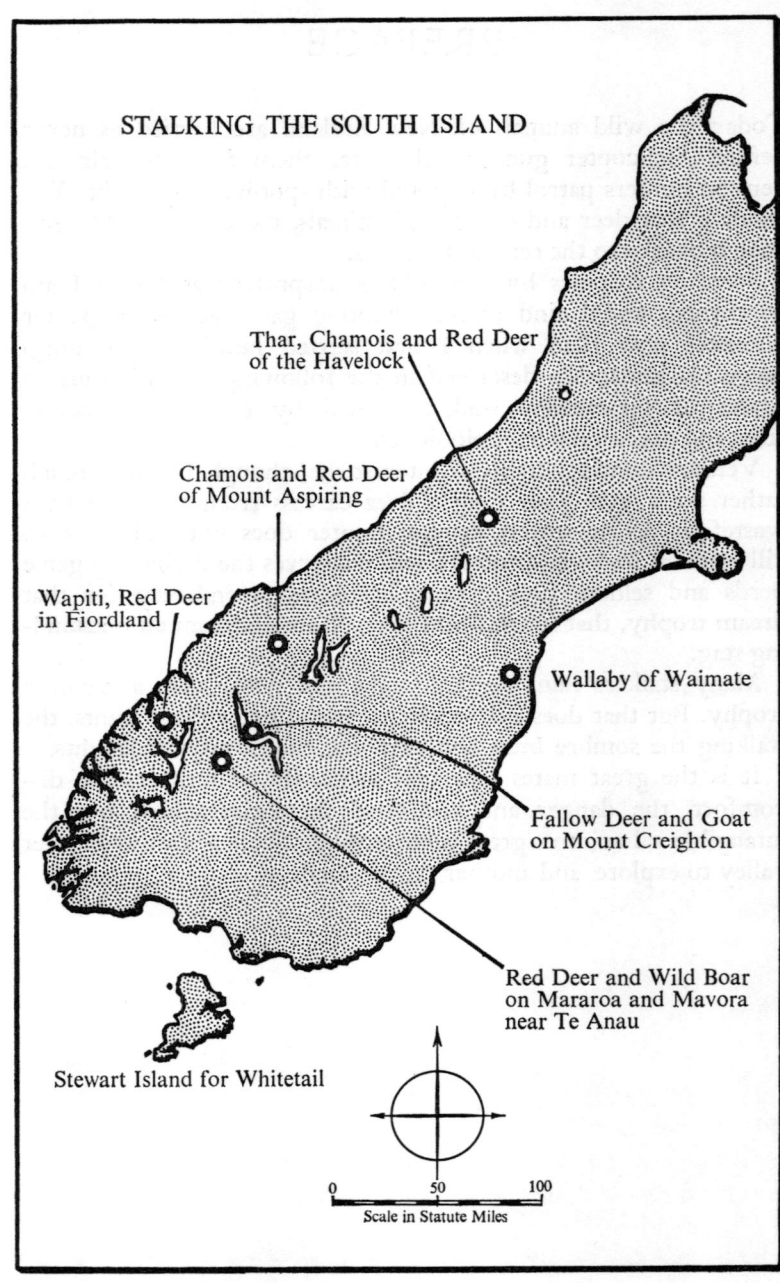

PART I
SOUTH ISLAND SAFARI

Hunters of the Havelock

An American Stalks the Southern Alps

THE HAVELOCK RIVER, swollen and discoloured, surged in one broad flood against the crumbling shingle bank. Perhaps the river crossing was negotiable by landrover, but it certainly wasn't inviting, even if an old set of ex-Army quad vehicle tracks did dive into the water nearby.

Wilby Oliver and I, of Hawke's Bay, had landed from the Wellington-Lyttelton Ferry at daylight that February morning and had met Mr William Koller of Pennsylvania at his hotel in Christchurch for breakfast. Bill Koller, who had flown in from the United States the previous day, was to be my guest in New Zealand on a hunting safari for the next three weeks. We had then discussed our plans for a leisurely drive down the South Island, stopping at likely spots for red and fallow deer, thar, chamois, wallaby, and pig.

As the vehicle had climbed through the high barren mountains of the Rangitata Gorge, the drought-stricken Canterbury Plains were left behind, with the rain-streaked ranges of the main Southern Alps appearing ahead. We had stayed a little while at Mesopotamia Station, talking with the manager, then crossed the arid river flats near the homestead and wound up the broad South Canterbury riverbed, dipping in and out of meandering sprawling streams, and skirting the worst and biggest shoals of boulders. About eleven miles above Mesopotamia the Rangitata River loses its identity, forking into two large snowfed rivers, the Havelock and the Clyde. We bumped the rover up the Havelock but not until the mouth of Carney Creek, some twenty-three miles upstream from Mesopotamia, did we meet the full volume of the Havelock in one great stream.

Groaning in lowest gear and four-wheel drive, distrustful of the deep ford, we backed off the Havelock and pioneered a new trail up boulder-strewn Carney Creek, then smashed across a wilderness of moss-covered rubble and scattered matagouri bushes up the Havelock. Once we tackled a shingle bank and grounded hard, one front wheel spinning in the air, but a little spadework and some shoulder weight from Bill and Wilby heaved us free.

Darkness, and an occasional rain squall, threatened as the lurching rover crawled up Forbes River, another major tributary of the Havelock, and crashed into the tumbling mountain torrent. Somehow the tough vehicle heaved its way through and over unseen boulders nearly as high as the wheels themselves, and crawled its way up the far bank. With Wilby and Bill ahead piloting a route, we weaved across Mistake Flats and came down to the deerstalkers' hut in the dusk. The cabin, two Army huts sandwiched together, huddled against a strip of moss-hung forest under the south-east corner of towering Mt MacMillan. Trees, bush, even a vigorous stand of scrub, is very rare in the bare shingle-scarred mountains of South Canterbury.

We were up early and away by 7 am, wading through the dew-drenched snowgrass as we turned into Forbes Valley. Where a cluster of moraine boulders spilled across the valley mouth we paused a moment to scan the great gorge ahead. Unlike the vast majority of mountain watersheds, Forbes runs straight for its entire length of some seven or eight miles, only forking to its twin glaciers right at the head under the sheer rock walls of 9,500-foot Mt d'Archiac.

Wilby spotted the stag first, standing in heavy shadow. I focussed the powerful binoculars, noted the wide spread and heavy cluster of points. The deer was just above the tussock, among scattered celery pine on the lower edge of a huge shingle slide. The range was long—400 yards at least, maybe further.

We were spotlighted by the rising sun behind and the stag had obviously seen us. Bill didn't hesitate. He scuttled to the nearest boulder, steadied the heavy rifle and fired once, then again and again as the stag spun and climbed slowly before turning across the distant slide. As the American's last shots hit rock, I muttered, "I'll turn him if I can."

By now the stag was 600 yards away, perhaps more. Aiming far ahead and above the beast, I touched off a string of quick shots, hoping to hold the stag while Bill reloaded and brought him down.

Undoubtedly hit by Bill's first shots, the stag paused by a dense thicket of scrub, then disappeared. Crying, "Come on Bill!" Wilby and I raced half a mile up the flat to watch the thicket. When the stag didn't re-appear, I climbed up the boulders, then struggled into the scrub to search.

A shot from Bill—he had spotted the stag moving ahead of me—missed. Scrambling atop a waist-high boulder I spotted great antlers weaving and swaying in the celery pine below, but couldn't shoot immediately. Two hundred yards below, Wilby and Bill were in line of fire so I waved and made aiming motions with my rifle. They dived behind a rock.

The stag was a lovely trophy, with antler length of left $40\frac{1}{4}''$, right $39\frac{1}{8}''$ and spread of $37\frac{1}{2}$ inches. Points fourteen, six on one side, eight on the other, where an extra forked throwback on one top denoted Rakaia blood. The tines were long and heavy, only just clean of velvet and lightly stained red with tanikaha pine. Incidentally, one bay tine had a nasty slash mark in it, where a bullet—probably one of mine as I tried to head him—had sliced through.

We spread the antlers and headskin on a jagged boulder, along with a generous portion of venison, then continued upstream and crossed to stalk the pleasant snowgrass slope which spills out below Easy Col. Deer are usually rather rare in the Havelock watershed, but there was some fresh sign about. With practically no cover, it is hard to understand where these deer ghost away to. While boiling the billy I swung my 20 X binoculars along the steep southern slope of Mt Oklahoma and spotted a large buck chamois. While we lunched the buck grazed, disappeared, then re-appeared on a commanding knob and settled to rest. High above the lone chamois, among the crags, were the first thar we had seen—three young bulls.

A mile from the chamois, we tried to cross the broad shingle stream bed, but the sharp-eyed buck spotted us and fled.

Late in the afternoon, Wilby climbed high above to search a steep, deep canyon which angles off the southern flank of Mt Oklahoma. During winter, avalanches plunge straight into it off the high peaks above, and it must almost fill with snow. Vegetation is sparse, but thar prefer these jagged rock walls and Wilby saw a number of nannies and kids, also two young bulls. Searching for a trophy bull, he didn't fire.

In the meantime Bill and I had spotted five chamois, females and kids, high above the steep strip of scrub which clings to the mouth of Forbes on the southern cliffs. Further along, on a ledge under a smooth rock bluff, one lone hind grazed in the evening sunlight. Three-quarters of a mile above us, quite inaccessible from above or below, we saw those same six animals several times again during the next few days. It had been over five years since I had last hunted the Havelock and chamois had decreased considerably since then.

Heavy driving rain discouraged an early start next day, but toward mid-morning we wandered north along the bush edge, looking for a spot to test Bill's rifle without disturbing the country too much. Leant against a rock the day before, the American's rifle had slipped and fallen heavily and he wanted to check the sensitive sight. The telescopic sight was an excellent Bausch & Lomb 2-8 Variable Power instrument, but windage and elevation adjustments were incorporated in the mounts, an unsatisfactory and easily displaced arrangement.

Where a rock slide spilled out below Mt MacMillan on to Mistake Flats, I set up an aiming mark, but before Bill could shoot the rain clouds parted so Wilby swung the binoculars along the cliffs of Mt MacMillan above the Lower Bench.

"There's a chamois," he exclaimed. Neither Wilby nor I were armed so we dashed to the hut for our rifles and hurried after Bill who was scaling a cascading waterfall, scrambling up to the shelf known as the Lower MacMillan Bench. The wind, a swirling damp blustering southerly, was unpleasant and probably warned the buck for he had disappeared. But I spotted another on the cliff to the right. We had stalked within 300 yards and were still creeping closer up a carved watercourse, when a chamois female and her kid leapt nimbly up the bluff, ricocheting from rock to rock past the buck and routing him. Bill fired two or three ineffectual shots as the chamois leapt from crag to crag, but didn't make a hit.

We carried on around Lower Bench for a mile, but the wind warned any game which might have been there. A couple of miles long and a half a mile wide, clothed in scattered thickets of scrub or tussock, the Lower Bench is a lovely spot for chamois and is also visited by an occasional deer. Oddly, thar do not frequent the Benches.

Angling high across the northern tussock shoulder of Mt MacMillan is the Upper Bench. From the higher shoulder there was a marvellous view to the distant headwaters of the Havelock and the high snow peaks of the Main Divide, but snow squalls and swirling fog discouraged further climbing.

Though it was raining heavily down the Havelock, after boiling the billy we waded the Forbes Stream and turned up the narrow defile of Murphy Creek. Murphy Creek lies south and parallel with Forbes. It is a remote and lonely valley, and a mile from the main Havelock Valley the Murphy Creek plunges over a high waterfall into a narrow craggy gorge filled with tough scrub. On an earlier visit I had climbed the falls into the Upper Murphy Valley when retrieving a fine chamois trophy, but don't recommend it. The route usually taken by the very occasional hunter is over Easy Col via the Forbes.

Hares are plentiful through all the tussock country of the South Island. As we turned into Murphy Gorge, a startled hare fled ahead of us, then panicked and went clawing up a cliff. We watched, fascinated at first, then apprehensive, as the hare leapt up the smooth rock walls, trying again and again as he scrambled from one tiny ledge to another. Forty feet up, clawing ineffectively as he slipped and lost balance the poor hare fell, bouncing and spinning off the jagged rocks. Not for a moment did we expect the hare to survive, but the brown furry animal picked itself up and without even a limp jogged downstream between Bill and myself.

Only forty or fifty yards further on, we edged round a bluff where the stream foamed between the boulders. A red deer hind eyed us from the scrub a little further on, so Bill Koller reached for my pack to grope for his movie camera.

Bill was a particularly keen and efficient movie photographer. In the landrover reposed a heavy and expensive Palliard Rolex 16 mm movie, complete with a battery of wide angle and telephoto lens. When hunting he preferred a smaller 16 mm movie, but it was a magazine film load which jammed frequently, usually when we had just completed a close-up stalk of wild game. That sort of camera trouble was extremely frustrating and disappointing. In addition, I always carried a pair of cameras and telelens of my own, one a 35 mm reflex loaded with colour film, the other a larger black and white 620 camera.

While running a movie sequence of the red hind, an inquisitive fawn joined its mother and presently the two deer went prancing up through the crags.

Bill's knee-high lace-up boots wouldn't stand up to river wading without serious shrinking, so Wilby splashed further up Murphy Gorge while Bill and I made our way along the steep scrubby slopes which face the Havelock. It should have been a likely place for a chamois trophy but we saw neither tracks nor droppings. A mile or so south two stags came trotting over the skyline high above, probably disturbed by Wilby.

A quick glance with the binoculars confirmed that neither were trophies, being merely a six and a long-tined eight-pointer respectively. Their fright over, the two stags slowed to a halt, looked and listened for a long period, then wandered across and down through the matagouri ahead of us, pausing for an occasional morsel. We pushed on towards them and the pair of deer froze, hiding in the scrub, watching apprehensively as we gradually approached. The stags didn't realise that though their bodies were concealed, their antlers poked above the low thorn bushes. A few chains away, they finally fled crashing through the scrub as Bill's movie whirred.

Late in the evening Bill and I climbed to a projecting shoulder, high above a lonely stand of birches. The American steadied his binoculars, focussed on a scrubby precipice and muttered: "There's an animal on that cliff. Must be a chamois but it looks sort of like a sheep, only it can't be."

It was a sheep though, a hungry, sorry Merino wether, stuck on a ledge and missed during the autumn muster some weeks previously. Though I tried I couldn't negotiate the cliff; a rope was needed so we reported the missing animal to Mesopotamia Station when we returned down-river.

Wilby tramped in behind us in the dusk. He had shot at a couple of thar but didn't bring them down. Rain lashed the hut again that evening as we sipped a whisky apiece while Bill showed us the photos of his two recent African safaris, both fabulously successful, to Portuguese Angola and Mozambique. There is no lure to compare with the trophy hunter's urge to go to the furthest corners of the earth in search of his game. It's a great life, out there, rifle in hand, whether in New Zealand's mountains, Africa's deserts, or the snowy wastes of the Arctic.

Chamois on the High Peaks

AT DAWN THE NEXT DAY, fresh and dew-laden, the three of us, Bill, Wilby, and myself headed up the wide Forbes Valley. Layers of grey fog shrouded the heights of the Cloudy Peaks Range to our rear but Mt d'Archiac, towering into the skies ahead of us, glistened white with fresh snow.

For the first mile or two we saw no game, until we edged over the moraine to stalk a little tussock hollow, fringed with gaunt snow-twisted scrub. Just above the celery pine thickets, where a vast gravel slide climbed steeply to the crags, stood a chamois, yellow in the young sunlight. Bill sprawled across a boulder, aimed carefully and fired. Three hundred yards away the chamois flinched, apparently mortally hit, then slowly picked its way up the shingle. Wilby didn't shoot, expecting the chamois to go down while I "called" Bill's shots through the binoculars. But though the American fired again and again, emptying his magazine, the chamois slowly climbed higher, gradually recovering strength and imperceptibly increasing the range.

While Bill groped for fresh shells I laid aside the 20 X binoculars and was shocked to see with the naked eye just how distant the chamois had become. Hastily I grabbed my 30.06, casting my eye about for an adequate aiming rest.

"What's the range, Wilby? Five hundred yards?"

"Nearer six."

Aiming a foot over the chamois' shoulder, I squeezed off. There was a perceptible instant while the bullet was in flight, then the chamois collapsed.

While Wilby and Bill Koller sat in the pleasant sun easing the dawn's chill from their bodies, I slogged up the mountain and raised a sweat. When I did reach Bill's trophy, I could barely distinguish my friends, they were so far away. Range was tremendous for the bullet I had aimed a foot over had hit the poor chamois in the lower front legs, a trajectory drop of three and a half feet. Long range musketry is justified to finish off wounded game, such as on this occasion, but often it is better to stalk closer first.

I dragged the chamois down the mountain, taking some care not to rip out a tendon in my leg with the two needle-sharp clawed horns. It was a female, a very old creature with fine long horns. Photos recorded, we left the trophy under a shaded rock and tramped on up the valley. Here and there great shingle slides spilled down from the tremendous peaks which wall in the valley. Directly above us reared the colossal pinnacle of Oklahoma Peak, just on 7,000 feet high, resplendent with hanging glaciers. The whole range plunges sheer almost to the valley floor.

A mile above us, hanging on a dizzy pinnacle in Oklahoma's shadow, four or five young bull thar nonchalantly grazed. Four were in their dark grey autumn coats, but one still sported a shaggy blond summer fur.

Further along, three chamois went leaping through a strip of extremely thick scrub and disappeared, half a mile ahead. We climbed on up the creek to where the Forbes Stream forked and wandered in among a maze of huge moraine boulders. Then we scrambled up the battered stones to a vantage point where annually the avalanches sweep down from Oklahoma's flanks.

While we ate lunch, washed down with occasional draughts of cold, fresh-melted snow water, the three of us glassed the surrounding peaks with our binoculars.

Without the aid of the powerful optical instruments there wasn't a beast in sight, but here and there distant game could be seen with the glasses. Across the moraine, at Mt d'Archiac's base, a great herd of thar, thirty or more, all nannies and kids, wandered among the rocks. Skylined on a bluff far up the opposite peak I spotted bull thar, big trophy beasts with heavy horns and great shaggy coats lapping the ground. After them we went, picking our way across the moraine, boulder-hopping both branches of Forbes Stream. Then up, slogging slowly straight up along the edge of a drifting shingle slide, climbing steeply like the rungs of an eternal endless ladder. Once there was a smattering of rolling rocks around us as three startled young thar scrambled across a crevasse high above. At last the three of us scrambled on to the scant tussock atop a bluff and peeped cautiously over the crest. The four bulls, when last seen, had been on another bluff much further round the mountain, but we had spied a well-worn game trail and intended edging through the crags, climbing across and above them.

Action came swiftly. There were bulls in sight and big trophies too, though not the animals we had climbed after. Eyeing us malevolently, intruders to his mountain castle, a huge bull thar stared up at us from the rocks below. Bill aimed his big rifle down between his feet, fired once and the bull collapsed. Another bull, slightly smaller, fled across the stones. Wilby fired, hit his target, and Bill and I each threw a shot at the wounded beast as it scrambled agilely across a bluff. Wilby descended to make certain of his first bull thar. He had hardly left us when four more bulls, our original quarry, dashed wildly across a scarred crag ahead. Bill and I aimed a shot or two their way, but they escaped. The gunfire disturbed more thar high above us, and one young bull leapt casually on to a pinnacle and stood calmly looking down at us from 800 feet above. Bill swung his rifle skyward, fired, but missed.

The American's bull thar was an excellent trophy, well-maned, and Wilby's was also a good animal. It was a long, long way back down the mountain to Forbes Stream so far below, and by the time we reached the hut in the dusk we had been tramping for over twelve hours.

At dawn next morning we left Mistake Flats Hut to stalk the MacMillan Benches for chamois. Thar seldom, if ever, invade these two huge ledges and red deer only occasionally, but chamois thrive there. Bill wanted a buck chamois to make a matched pair with the female he had shot the day before, and Wilby had never shot chamois at all.

It was a glorious morning, sun glistening on the dew-drenched bushes. The Lower Bench lies some seven or eight hundred feet above the river. Scattered stunted bushes, olearia, flax and manuka, dot the area, while high above rears the massive bulk of Mt MacMillan.

With the breeze in our favour, we patiently stalked the Lower Bench, but not an animal did we see, so we scrambled up another 1,000 feet via the only route—a winding game trail beside a waterfall—to the Upper Bench, a snowgrass plateau, two miles long and a mile wide, which angles across the sunny north shoulder of Mt MacMillan.

Stalking the Upper Bench six years before, I had seen a little herd of deer, and was hopeful to see some more, but there wasn't a dropping or hoof mark of deer on the whole Bench this time.

Chamois too were not in evidence and we had tramped a mile

round under the bluffs before the first game of the day was sighted. Six hundred yards above, on a snowgrass shoulder, five chamois wandered into view, then looked down at us. A chamois, by the way, has excellent eyesight and these spotted us instantly, though we were lying quietly, half-hidden in snowgrass. Buck chamois are rather solitary animals, very rarely more than two being seen together. The group above were female, but though Bill wasn't interested Wilby was.

A moment later a fine buck chamois came round the cliff high ahead. The beast saw us and sprang up the bluff before Bill could shoot. Poised on the summit, the buck paused. Bill fired and the buck reeled away as if hard hit.

Convinced Bill had filled his bag and taken the buck he coveted, we climbed up through the snowgrass, winding under and over the steep crags which dot the whole mountain.

There was no sign whatever of the chamois Bill had fired at!

We scrambled round the northern bluffs of Mt MacMillan into the teeth of a cold nor'wester that had sprung to life and was piling rain and snow squalls over the Divide.

The Upper Bench is sharply defined on the western rim, where a steep gorge drops from the top of the range and disappears to the Havelock thousands of feet below.

Crouching in the wind-lashed snowgrass we searched for game, but could see nothing, so Wilby and Bill Koller finally fired a couple of shots apiece, splitting a white rock up the chasm. There was quite a long pause, then two disturbed thar came toiling up from somewhere away beneath, then panicked and dived madly across the erosion-scarred gully. Neither were trophies and never would be, for the three of us sent a volley of lead at the fleeing animals, and brought both of them down at a dead run at over 300 yards' range. There are plenty of thar in the Havelock without having them invade the MacMillan Benches. Incidentally, noteworthy of the Upper Bench is a profusion of the lovely Mt Cook lily.

There is a spectacular cliff, two, perhaps three, thousand feet high on the outer rim of the Upper Bench, where it plunges sheer to the Havelock River. Chamois occasionally flit about the ledges and rock chimneys of the precipice, but the boisterous wind made the cliff-edge dangerous. Toward evening we wandered down, descending to the river and hut.

During the night rain and wind slashed savagely at our whare, and it was a wet and sodden dawn, with rain still pouring down. By noon the weather was clearing, so we walked up the nearby Forbes Valley. A few chamois were sighted, high on the mountain above, but they either watched from a safe 1,000 yards or else went leaping away.

The Forbes River was quite high—a dirty grey-yellow colour —so instead of wading it we climbed the short steep spur which Wilby had investigated a day or two before. Very high on the sheer southern walls of Mt Oklahoma we saw thar, way off, quite a few of them, but all were nannies and kids, scattered in small mobs.

Directly below the peak a great pile of dirty snow, remnants of last winter's avalanches, still filled a hidden chasm. From the black, scarred cliff above, a solid stream of water gushed straight out of the solid rock, and went splashing down under the avalanche beneath.

While we had a bite to eat and planned next day's stalk, a pair of friendly keas fluttered down to visit us.

The evening was fine and clear, so cheerfully we planned one last big hunt for the morrow on the heights between Murphy Creek and Forbes. But it was a drear morning with steady rain next day, snow low on the surrounding mountains and more piling up with every squall. The turbulent Havelock was coming up fast, building up to a full flood, and the sooner we got downriver with the landrover the better. Instead of trying to backtrail the shocking route we had blazed coming in, we followed a faint jeep trail out across Mistake Flats to the river. Split into five foaming channels the Havelock looked formidable, dangerous even, at its likeliest crossing. With the extension exhaust fitted and a tarpaulin secured under and up over the motor, we churned into the flood, rocking and bouncing and rolling over unseen boulders two feet high. Somehow, the rover smashed its way across, crawling dripping out the far side.

For miles we weaved down the river shingle, grinding in low four-wheel drive, congratulating ourselves on avoiding so many river crossings.

Then trouble! The whole great Havelock River, a swollen yellow flood, swung across our path and hurled into a bluff ahead. It was rising every moment; even as we searched desperately for a crossing it spread across new channels, cold yellow fingers of water seeking out the lower surfaces and lapping across the gravel.

At the likeliest place we could see, I swung the rover into the flood. The vehicle dipped sharply off the bank, slithering into the river, angling down so steeply it seemed we would go clean under. Yellow water surged across the top of the bonnet, then even the spare wheel atop the bonnet disappeared under the river. I kept my foot hard down on the petrol, fighting the wheel, knowing that if the engine died we'd have a job swimming out of it. Water surged up level with the window and the drive felt light, as if the rover was almost afloat, drifting down-river.

Water inside the cab was up to our knees, filling the top of Bill's high-laced American boots. Then we were in midstream where the river was shallower. Only another ten yards to go and we splashed out on to the shingle.

The motor choked, spluttered, died. The distributor was full of water. But we were safe, temporarily at least, with only another fifty, sixty, perhaps a hundred crossings ahead between us and Mesopotamia. In twenty minutes the motor had dried itself out so impatiently we bounced down-river, haunted by the rising flood in the eighteen miles of riverbed still ahead.

Below Growler Hut we were hugging the Mesopotamian bank, making better time, when a chamois came leaping out of a hidden gorge 150 yards up the mountain.

Bill, who had been cradling his .300 Magnum, leapt out, fired, and hit the buck rather low in the knee. The chamois ran over a rise. Frantically I tore the truck canopy aside, groping for my rifle, then sprinted upstream after my companions. Far up the mountain the chamois re-appeared, a distant tiny target, limping badly. Then Bill's rifle was empty and I had only one shot left and the truck half a mile away. The chamois climbed gamely up a watercourse, scrambled on to a bluff and vanished 800 yards above us.

Puzzled we watched and waited, finally deciding that the animal had holed up. I detoured round the mountain, climbing high and steep across the slope, and finally stepped cautiously out to the crest of the crag and peered over. Fifty feet below me the buck lay in a shallow cavern, wounded and hiding. I fired once, my last cartridge, and the buck rolled, bouncing and careering until I was certain the precious horns would be smashed. But Bill had his buck chamois, by some freak of the hunting gods, and a lovely trophy it was too. Over nine inches long, heavy and black, the chamois was very old, with teeth entirely worn away.

Just before evening we forged through the flood for the last time. The journey had taken four hours going in, nine coming out from Mistake Flats to Birch Creek. As we drove into Timaru the following morning there was a horrible grating crunching noise in the rear end. One wheel bearing had cut out.

Wallabies of Waimate

THE BIG GREY WALLABY whirled and fled, springing effortlessly into the scraggy thorn bushes as the rover whined into view. In four-wheel drive we rattled on up the damp clay track, reversed and turned where the trail degenerated into a sheep track and disappeared in the sombre bush.

Our wheel bearing replaced, we were now scouring Mt Studholme in the Hunter Hills south-west of Timaru.

Our weapons were diverse. Bill Koller cradled his heavy .300 Holland and Holland Magnum; Wilby handled a .303 S.M.L.E., and I, as guide, not expecting to do any shooting, had picked up a scarred Remington .22 rim-fire from the gun rack.

There were a few stale wallaby droppings in the first strip of bush, and more away along the snowgrass ridge, but we had gone a mile or more before game was sighted again. To both left and right the valleys were choked with bush, green fingers of lush growth reaching high into the snowgrass mountains ahead. The three of us slipped through the drenched tussock and came on a group of wallaby below on a little stony knoll in the bush fringe. A couple of small ones were carelessly chasing each other among the flax bushes while three or four more grazed the short sparse grass. When Bill's cannon boomed out a heavy grey wallaby went down. As the startled creatures leapt in confusion the

American fired again but missed. Intrigued by the strange-looking animal he had shot Bill ran down to his kill, turned it over, smoothed the fur and remarked: "This sure is the most odd-ball sort of a critter I ever did shoot."

Wallaby *are* odd animals. Their powerful heavy hind legs, balanced by a thick three-foot tail, support only a frail chest and delicate front paws. Actually the front shoulder, paws and head of a wallaby look much like an opossum and aren't much larger. Both marsupials originated from Australia and carry their young in pouches, but a mature wallaby, such as Bill Koller's, must weigh nigh on fifty pounds. The fur is very similar to opossum, but though they can be skinned while warm, they are tough punching.

I handled Bill's 16 mm camera for a session of movie-making, then ran off half a dozen black and white and coloured photos before taking the entire pelt off ready for a full life-size wallaby mount for Bill's trophy room.

While slipping the fur into my pack I glanced across the valley to see four more wallaby swirling in and out of the bush, playing tag, each following exactly the twisty course of the leader. There was half a mile of damp bush to traverse, but when we stepped warily on to the spur our four wallaby had departed.

With a blunt pocket knife a tin of salmon was hacked open and we lunched on the ridge, pausing occasionally to swing the glasses along the fringes of the bush and on to a rocky outcrop that thrust above the trees. Now and then, a wallaby would dart into view or hop casually about grazing.

For a few years the shooting of wallaby had been barred while the Forestry Department poured tons of 1080 poison from the sky in an extermination campaign. Certainly the wallaby of South Canterbury once required drastic curtailment, but now the shooting ban had been lifted there still appeared to be plenty of wallaby left.

Wilby now took the lead, stalking a little ahead with his .303. Four or five hundred yards away beyond a forested valley we could see half a dozen wallaby, so we kept under cover of the matipo and whitey-wood trees along the bush edge. Considerable caution is needed to close in on these marsupials, for they have an exceedingly keen eye.

Bill and I froze as Wilby's rifle came swinging up, aimed—then the sharp click of a misfire. Quietly my mate ejected the defective cartridge and bolted another shell into the breech. This time the .303 fired, and a large wallaby dived past headlong downhill into the bush.

Before trailing Wilby's wallaby, a movement on a distant rocky bluff caught my eye. The glasses showed a small wallaby crouching under the fern. Quite invisible to the naked eye, Bill twisted his Varipower rifle scope to its full magnification and grabbed my frame pack for a rest. A long pause . . . the American's Winchester 70 recoiled and the wallaby slithered sideways—dead. It was a pretty piece of shooting.

Wilby spied another pair of the animals on a rock some 300 yards up the gorge. With the open-sighted .303 he couldn't even see his target, so Bill thrust the big .300 into his hands. Wilby winged his quarry at the first shot, then fired two or three times again in a vain attempt to kill the wallaby, but the animal—apparently only grazed by the bullet—finally hopped into the trees.

Searching the bush for the wallaby Wilby had fired at with his .303 we found a blood trail that soon disappeared, so we spread to quarter a wider area. There was no undergrowth in this low forest, for sheep and wallaby had trimmed any seedlings. It must have been nearly half an hour before Bill shouted triumphantly, dragging Wilby's kill from where it had pitched dead behind a log. Shot cleanly through the shoulder with a solid nose .303 bullet, the animal still travelled over 100 yards before going down.

While Bill and I crossed the gorge to skin his second kill, Wilby went on to try and track the wallaby he had lightly scratch-wounded. A lamb was bawling distractedly in the gorge below, so the American and I climbed down to see if it needed help. The lamb was long-tailed, clean-eared, and while we watched its mother, a double-decker fleeced hermit ewe, picked its way through the bush to reclaim its lost lamb. The wool of both sheep was full of leaves, and they obviously lived in the depths of the forest, shunning their kind and foraging for fresh-fallen leaves.

While examining Bill's trophy we heard several wallaby approaching through the trees, fleeing Wilby's approach higher up the valley. Thump, thump, thump, a pair slipped past, above and below us, then another leapt to the rocks above. Bill shot and the wallaby came tumbling down.

Late in the evening we plodded through the bush, crossing a wide tree-filled valley towards our vehicle. Two wallaby darted through the gloomy forest, paused, and my .22 spoke once. The little hollow-nose bullet dropped the wallaby instantly and, in fact, ruined the skin completely.

By the landrover the rifles were all unloaded and shells placed in packs or pockets, when an unfortunate wallaby was so unwary as to appear across a rocky gully. The American, quite content with his three fine skins, handed his .300 Magnum to Wilby.

Wilby sprawled in the gorse bushes, squeezed off and bowled the last wallaby.

Fallow Deer of Mt Creighton

AFTER OUR SUCCESSFUL WALLABY HUNT Wilby was called back to the north, while Bill and I drove the landrover further south, across the Lindis Pass and down towards Queenstown. From there we hoped to acquire a trophy from the herds of nimble fallow deer on Mt Creighton.

Until very recently, Mt Creighton Station, halfway up Lake Wakatipu on the eastern shore, had been accessible only by launch or float plane, but the new route to Glenorchy had ended the remote quiet of this station. A steady stream of nervous tourists now idled past, and battered landrovers, laden with venison from the Dart and Rees, pounded back and forth to Queenstown.

Bill and I had a yarn to Mr Keyes senior, the owner, who genially suggested we base camp in the shearers' quarters. Mr Keyes remarked that good fallow bucks were scarce, particularly hard to find so early in the season, before the rut. Mustering the week before, their dogs had disturbed a pair of fine bucks from a strip of birch bush high on the distant slopes of Mt Creighton. Having had some previous experience of guiding Americans and knowing their aversion to back-packing, I was happily surprised when Bill turned to me.

"Well Keith, I've never carried a pack in my life, but if that's the only way to shoot a fallow buck, looks as if I'll have to start today!"

Fifty-nine years old is a little late to introduce a new hunter to the heavy pack and the long trail, but Bill was tough, and getting leaner and keener every day. A few days later, 4,000 feet above the lake, Bill was to mutter: "I'm beginning to know why these guys like Hillary climb mountains. It's just to see what's over the top. What say you and I climb that mountain?" pointing to a wind-lashed crag on the skyline towering another 2,000 feet above.

I spent the next hour sorting supplies and stuffing gear into a couple of rucksacks. Bill carried a pair of sleeping bags while I humped sufficient food supplies for four days, plus tent and billies.

Sweating, panting, the two of us slogged straight up the mountain, winding up through the belt of bracken fern into the short windswept tussock. The view was absolutely glorious, giving frequent excuse to swing aside the packs and reach for our cameras. Directly below, Mt Creighton homestead was hidden by a grove of birches, but its pleasant vari-coloured fields, partitioned by wandering forested streams, were delightful. A couple of offshore islets, Pig and Pigeon Islands, supported a few sheep, and a thin grey smoke screen above one island indicated autumn burning in progress. To the westward I pointed out the Greenstone and Caples Valleys beyond the lake, haunt of other herds of elusive fallow.

From a shoulder high on the slopes of Mt Creighton peak we surveyed the sheltered basin which swept across the northern face of the crag. A thousand acres of birch forest sprawled across the valley, fingers of beech pushing up the mountain, but above the forest there was a magnificent sweep of snowgrass pasture.

Our first sign of fallow deer was a weathered set of old antlers whitening at the bush edge. Then I almost stepped on a little black doe, sound asleep in the snowgrass. She leapt frantically for cover. Further on I saw another deer sunning itself on the forest fringes as I crept over a rock. I drew slowly back, turned and gesticulated to the American to unlimber his movie.

Where a tiny mountain stream wandered into the forest I set up the cramped 7 x 4 tent, and strung the fly over it. Then Bill cut bundles of snowgrass for bedding while I gathered firewood and rocks for a fireplace. Perched on a commanding rock above the timberline, we watched the shadows of evening spilling across the valley. There were a few fallow deer in sight, odd little bands of does and fawns, usually three or four in a group, but of bucks we saw no sign. Some of the deer were miles and miles distant, caught momentarily by the failing sun, magnified by our binoculars. There were also half a dozen goats, multi-coloured nannies and kids, bleating on the bluffs above.

Before dawn next morning Bill and I were climbing through the snowgrass, soaked waist-high with dew. We saw and crept past the same small bands of fallow deer, still grazing close to the friendly bush. Once we paused to watch as an impatient fawn vigorously suckled its mother, lifting the fond doe almost off its feet. The American and I climbed steadily and by ten o'clock were only a quarter of a mile from the high rim of the snowgrass basin when four red stags filed on to the skyline above. A light breeze swirling across had warned them. I whipped up the glasses, glimpsed the leading beast and exclaimed: "The first is a six. Second stag has only one antler. Here comes the third, he's the best head, a big ten-pointer. The last is an eight-pointer."

Bill aimed his rifle hurriedly but the deer vanished. I consoled him by remarking that the range was long and that his big fourteen-point red was a far better trophy. But Bill, not a killer by any means, replied, "Just in case anything happened to the head and headskin I'd like a second specimen."

Climbing on to the crest after the stags, we came on a large ugly billy goat with a fair horn spread. A few years ago goats were everywhere on Creighton, but a vigorous culling campaign by the Southland Deerstalkers' Association had reduced goat numbers considerably. I studied the Angora with the glasses and whispered to Bill to take him. Hit with the 180-grain bullet, the billy plunged lifeless off his perch, rolling toward a crevasse. Frightened, another billy goat leapt on to the rocks.

"Shoot that one too, Bill," I suggested. "It's a better trophy than the other." The second goat dropped as the heavy gunshot boomed out to echo across the placid lake.

We collected the horns from the second billy, but Bill preferred the brown fur for mounting, so we switched capes. With horns and skin in my pack we slogged up through the snowgrass under a boiling noonday sun. We aimed for a low, sharp little saddle to our left, but a spur of rock, craggy and crumbling, forced us higher until finally we stumbled out to the shoulder high above where the red stags had disappeared hours before. To the east, a rough snowgrass valley, steep and scarred, dropped away to drain into Moke Lake. On our right there was a wide tussock hollow, shimmering with heat haze. We were straddling the watershed, probably around 5,500 feet, for Mt Creighton, 6,500 feet, was less than 1,000 feet above us, close by to the south. The two of us relaxed and after a little we both removed our damp boots and sat yarning among the tall tussock.

Perhaps half an hour went pleasantly by before I stood up and stepping warily, watching for speargrass in my bare feet, inspected the great mountain gorge again. Instantly I spotted the fallow buck, grazing placidly in the basin some three or four hundred yards below. It was a broiling hot midday, and to see a fine trophy deer in that time and place was incredible. As the binoculars focussed I gasped, "Bill, there's a fallow buck and he's a beauty."

The American began searching the snowgrass frantically for his .300 Magnum.

"Find your boots before you shoot, Bill. Get your boots on."

As I hauled on my hobnailed, unlaced boots, Bill demanded his favourite aiming support, which was my tall frame pack. The basin between our vantage point and the buck was completely open—we couldn't stalk closer—so having seen Bill do some excellent long-range shooting previously I didn't argue.

As the gunshot boomed out, the bullet struck just beyond the stag, a few inches high. The buck came bounding toward us, running wild like a stampeding stallion before a fire. With his magnificent sweep of antlers the animal looked spectacular. For a brief second he halted on the edge of a water-torn crevasse, but before the hunter could shoot once more he leapt across and was galloping under the bluff below. Briefly, directly beneath, the buck stopped again as Bill fired. There was a hollow "bonk" but the fallow was off again, running madly.

"Shoot ahead and turn him, Keith!"

But already the stag was out of sight. I sprinted down across the tussock ridge, leaping rocks and speargrass bushes in desperate haste. As I dashed on to a rocky outcrop the stag came charging across below me, mouth wide open, antlers lapping back, making frantically for the snowgrass saddle and safety just ahead. Before I could shoot, the stag had dashed beyond another spine of rim rock. I leapt to the crest and saw the buck just below me, bounding for the ridge. I flung up the rifle, pulled the trigger, and heard the dull click of a defective cartridge savagely. I slammed the bolt open and levered another shell into the breech. Only twenty yards to go and the buck would be gone for ever. I fired, and the gallant buck crumpled in mid-stride. I turned, surprised at the disappointed voice of Bill Koller behind me.

"Keith," he gasped, "I was just going to shoot again when you dropped him. I like to finish all my own kills if I can."

While the American hobbled back to pick up his boots, I remarked that I didn't see how he could possibly have rushed across a couple of hundred yards of mountain, barefoot, in the time he did. Bill was the original good keen man all right.

The fallow carried an even head of sixteen points, long and very wide. Palmation was fair but not heavy. Curiously enough, one antler was clean of velvet and polished but the left antler was still covered in velvet, and I don't believe it would ever have shed, as there was no coronet developing about part of the base.

The buck was in extremely good condition, carrying a thick layer of fat. Heavily laden with meat and trophies, we climbed back to the crest of the range, then while I spent an hour or more caring for the headskins Bill carried on along the knife-edge ridge for another mile.

By 6 pm we were in camp, venison stew simmering and steak sizzling in the frypan. In the light of the flickering, fitful campfire I fleshed out the two headskins while Bill foraged for more snowgrass to lift himself off the birch roots and boulders.

The venison stew made a quick and nourishing breakfast and before sun-up we were away from camp. Fog, dense, damp, and grey, billowed up from Lake Wakatipu, receded, then settled across Mt Creighton's crown. We climbed back toward the hunting ground of the previous day, intending to stalk far along the range, but the fog swirling down halted us occasionally. By 11 o'clock the sun was shafting through, brightening sombre bush or yellow snowgrass, but then strident voices and shrill barks ahead advertised the appearance of autumn musterers on their beat.

We glassed the mountains around, but there was no game in sight, even the stray goat disappearing towards crag or forest before the dogs' distant cry. Leisurely we descended to camp, ate lunch, and then packed up. Though there was ample food, salt for headskins was short, and another thing, ominous thunderheads were building up in the mountains north and west about the Dart and the Greenstone.

We skidded off the mountain, descending to the fields and homestead so far beneath. By nightfall, cold rain and sleet were drenching lake and mountain. Bill and I spent a pleasant evening at the homestead with the station owners, viewing Bob Keyes's slides of the Mt Creighton area. Their sheep station sprawls for 45,000 acres, carries 8,000 Merino sheep and some cattle, plus sundry fallow deer, goats, and a visiting red deer or two.

All next day the rain continued, but toward darkness Bill and I explored the new road to Glenorchy in the rover.

Snow, fresh and undisturbed, softened the peaks of Creighton as the American and I left the Keyes and drove south, heading for new hunting territory in Southland.

Boar at Bay

COLD DRIVING RAIN lashed the rover as we slithered and churned down the Mararoa trail. The vehicle lurched out of a hollow, then skidded sideways through the mud as I tramped hard on the brakes.

I grabbed the binoculars, dragged the perspex window impatiently aside, and focussed on the great black animal up the slope. Dimly seen through the storm, for a moment I thought it was a black cattle beast. Half-buried in the hole he had rooted out, the pig turned and lifted his head.

"Shoot him, Bill," I breathed. "It's a monster."

Bill Koller was reluctant.

"Mr Bradley said I wasn't to shoot any pigs here."

"Shoot, Bill," I pleaded. "Allan Bradley wasn't talking about pigs like that one."

Still the American wasn't convinced.

"Bill," I said emphatically, "if you don't shoot that pig, I'm going to!"

Slowly Bill climbed from the rover.

Two hundred and fifty yards up the tussock slope the huge boar still churned the black wet soil, for the storm effectively concealed our presence.

Bill's .300 Holland and Holland Magnum roared and recoiled as the pig turned sideways. Mortally hit, the animal staggered ten or twelve feet, then slumped dead.

Bill and I pushed through the waist-high snowgrass to inspect the kill. The pig was enormous, with great white fangs curving far out of the jaw.

"I've never seen a wild boar as big as this," I said to Bill, "—let alone shot one!"

"I don't know what Mr Bradley will say," said Bill unhappily.

Bill and I had arrived at Mararoa Station, down Te Anau way, late the previous evening. To the south a snowstorm, black and menacing, was lashing the Takitimu Mountains. Far to the north another squall was swirling around the mountains of Mavora, but at the homestead the sun shone occasionally. Allan Bradley, owner of the sprawling Mararoa sheep station, was at the local dog trials, so Bill and I had a yarn to Fred, the station cook, tossed our gear into the shearers' quarters, and headed away to fish the Mararoa River.

A mile or so north of the woolshed we set up our rods and left the rover to tramp down to the distant river.

We hadn't gone 100 yards when I was surprised to note fresh pig-rooting among the tussock. There wasn't any bush for cover within three or four miles, not even a decent patch of fern or matagouri. I'm afraid the pig-rooting put me right off fishing. Since neither of us carried a rifle, I felt stark naked.

We fished for an hour or two but neither of us got a touch, though I used a series of wet flies, and Bill a bait caster. A frustrating feature was the sight of several trout feeding in the clear, swift river, and quite oblivious of our lures.

Back at Mararoa Allan swung his Holden in to greet us. I

American hunter W. Koller looks down the Forbes Valley, across the Havelock to the distant Cloudy Peak Range in South Canterbury.

Bill Koller with his fourteen-point stag shot in the Forbes.

A bull thar shot in South Canterbury by American Bill Koller.

This wallaby from the Hunter Hills fell to rifleman W. Koller.

remarked about the newly-turned earth upstream.

"Don't you go shooting my tame pigs up there now," Allan Bradley said.

I knew all about the "tame" pigs on Mararoa, so figured Allan was letting an old wild sow raise a litter or two unmolested. Before I could speak, Allan continued:

"Got a really big tusker all lined up for Bill here. Out on the hill above Dawson City. The dogs have had him bailed three times now, but I've called them off, leaving him until you got here."

Allan went on to describe a particularly horrible clump of matagouri thorns that the boar frequented. With a wicked twinkle Allan generously remarked that he would give Bill, as the American guest, the honour of crawling into the matagouri with the dogs, knife in his mouth, to administer the coup-de-grâce.

Allan and his two shepherds were drafting cattle next day so at daylight Bill and I bumped past the woolshed and headed upstream to try for the rainbow trout of lovely Lake Mavora, some thirty miles distant. Soon rain was slashing in from the south, streaming down the windscreen and flooding the dirt track in a yellow torrent. Fishing was out of the question. An obscure set of wheel marks strayed up a snowgrass valley to the west. I slowed the rover and we bounced into the storm.

There was sudden excitement as a stag went leaping through the tussock not far ahead. Bill scooped up his rifle and I snatched the binoculars, but already the stag had disappeared in the rain.

The trail wandered across a wide swampy basin, known as Sawmill Gully. I saw a mark to the left, and levered the rover into it. The truck lurched, recovered, then slowed and shuddered to a halt, tipped almost on its side.

The mark I had glimpsed through the rain-streaked windscreen was a deep drain off to one side of the track. Since the lower door wouldn't open, Bill clambered across a motley collection of firearms and cameras and out my side. The right front wheel, still slowly spinning, was a good six inches clear of the track, but the chassis was firmly grounded for its entire length.

After an hour's digging and scraping beneath the belly of the rover, I gunned the motor once more while Bill heaved on the bonnet. This time the wheels skidded, grabbed, and we squelched out of the ditch.

Mobile again but somewhat wary of Sawmill Gully, we skidded back up the Mararoa track. Where the main trail fords the river on the way to Burwood, there is an isolated strip of birch forest crowning the hill above the road. A sheltered, likely spot for deer, and sure enough, two stags stood watching us from the bush fringes. Bill scanned them with his binoculars and muttered that the largest was a ten-pointer. The American's favourite aiming rest was across the bonnet of the rover, but when Bill unfastened his door the two deer promptly moved into the trees and were lost.

Allan Bradley's instructions regarding the Mararoa ford were simple. "There is a big rock about a third way out. If you can see it, don't attempt to straddle it, or you'll ground and stay there like Bill Hazlett did. If you can't see the rock, don't cross, because the river is too deep anyway."

The rock was barely visible, with the Mararoa still rising rapidly. Loath to spend a wet day around camp, Bill and I headed the rover into the storm again, exploring an adjacent snowgrass basin known as The Chimneys. The little tussock creek was in full flood, one crossing swirling waist-deep. I fitted the extension exhaust and covered the radiator with a tent fly and the rover surged through like an amphibian tank.

The Chimneys showed no fresh sign of either pig or deer, so after two hours' stalking the birch fringes, Bill and I headed back to the homestead.

During the afternoon the storm still continued. It was as rough a day as I've ever seen. Busy checking and salting a chamois headskin, I was somewhat surprised when around four o'clock Bill remarked that perhaps the ten-pointer up the Mararoa would be worth looking for again. No doubt about it, Bill was keen enough.

We donned our parkas, headed the rover upriver, but the stags had more sense than to face the southerly. Returning to camp just on dark, we came on the huge boar and shot it as already described.

With considerable difficulty, Bill and I dragged the boar down to the truck and manoeuvred it aboard.

Allan was talking to Fred, the cook, and Ron, the shepherd, when I braked at the homestead.

"Better have a look at the sucking pig Bill has shot," I remarked.

"Where did you shoot that pig?" Allan demanded.

"Upriver, past the end of the ploughing," I replied.

"You've gone and shot my tame boar," stormed the station owner.

Ron, not to be outdone in leg pulling, fingered the boar's scarred ear, slashed with fighting. "Look at the Mararoa ear-mark."

"Why did you shoot my stud boar?" thundered Allan.

"Keith said to shoot so I shot," said poor Bill Koller.

Weighed on the woolshed scales, the boar turned 238 pounds. It was extremely fat with a heavy shield.

Fully convinced of his guilt, it was two days before Bill realised he had really shot the grandad of all wild boars. Incidentally, the same boar had been a menace the previous spring, having developed a taste for fresh-born lambs. Allan had only seen the pig in action on one occasion and had failed to bail him.

Snow that night cleared the weather, so the following afternoon, in two jeeps, we left the homestead and climbed past Lake Thomas. Perched atop a snowgrass plateau, rimmed by flax, the shallow lake is a favoured Southland fishing spot. A few miles beyond Lake Thomas Allan directed Ron and me aside to climb a high tussock ridge. With rifles and a dog we were to guard the head of two scrubby gullies, in case another big boar fled our way, or more likely, a deer was flushed from the birches.

A mile above the larger party, Ron and I watched as the dogs quested fruitlessly, back and forth, through the matagouri, in and out the birches.

Actually there was some very fresh pig sign high on the spur, and once or twice Ron's dog put his head in the air, then darted aimlessly toward the scrub. With a full pack to give him courage, I don't doubt we would have found pigs, but before we could go down and contact the main party they climbed into their vehicle and bumped off to search another area.

Trailing the tyre marks through the fern and snowgrass an hour later Ron and I located the other party's rover. It was parked by a winding gully dotted with occasional birches among the fern. Mrs Bradley, with her two sons, was waiting there, together with Jack, a visitor. As a matter of fact, every man, woman and child on Mararoa Station except Fred the cook was out pighunting that Sunday afternoon.

A few minutes previously, Mrs Shirley Bradley had heard a distant barrage of shots, when the dogs startled three deer from the gorge.

Suddenly there was pandemonium. The dogs had located a boar upstream, not half a mile away. Barking, yelping, we could hear the fray as the squealing pig plunged through the scrub. Joe, the other station shepherd, appeared on top of a gravel bank bellowing:

"Hold him! Hold him!"

Allan roared: "Bring the rope."

Everybody, including Mrs Bradley and the two boys aged four and five years, dashed for the scene of action.

The boar, a fairly large black animal, was bailed in shallow water, backed against a gravel bank, tormented by half a dozen grinning dogs. As we arrived he charged through the pack. Mrs Bradley snatched a youngster aside as the boar tore past but the chances of going under the team of excited hounds was almost as great. The boar bailed again, this time in a dense thicket of matagouri. Grinning and thoroughly enjoying himself, Bill Koller manoeuvred with his big movie camera, while I crawled in with a pair of still cameras.

The boar rushed a dog, sent him yelping, then fled upstream again to bail against the bank. It was an excellent place to take that rather rare photograph of a wild boar at bay. Then Allan and Ron were in the mêlée, grabbing a leg apiece to tip the boar on his back. Allan was determined to rope the boar and take him home alive and kicking. One of the dogs was robbed of his collar to use as a muzzle, buckled just above the tusks, but that didn't stay on long. There are dog collars all up and down that creek now!

Roped and back on his feet, the boar still wouldn't give in. Instead he charged the two men on the rope. Allan jumped aside, but Ron was too slow and the boar dashed clean between his legs. Ron still wonders what would have happened if his legs hadn't been well spread. Trailing the rope, the boar was soon bailed again. Half a dozen times in the next hilarious hour the pig alternately sulked, charged, escaped, was bailed again; then was roped and finally lifted into the sheep crate aboard the land-rover trailer.

By the back gate of Mararoa homestead that evening half a dozen of us grabbed the boar, then held hard while Allan earmarked him, then performed a couple of surgical operations with a sharp knife. As that very annoyed and justifiably angry big ex-boar scrambled to his feet, half a dozen men leapt aside quickly.

Even Big Bill Hazlett from Burwood, who is a heavy man indeed, was on the bonnet of his rover in one jump.

"Say, Allan, you're not going to let that boar go right here, are you?" I asked.

"Certainly! You're putting on a film show in here tonight and we must liven things up for the visitors!"

We did!

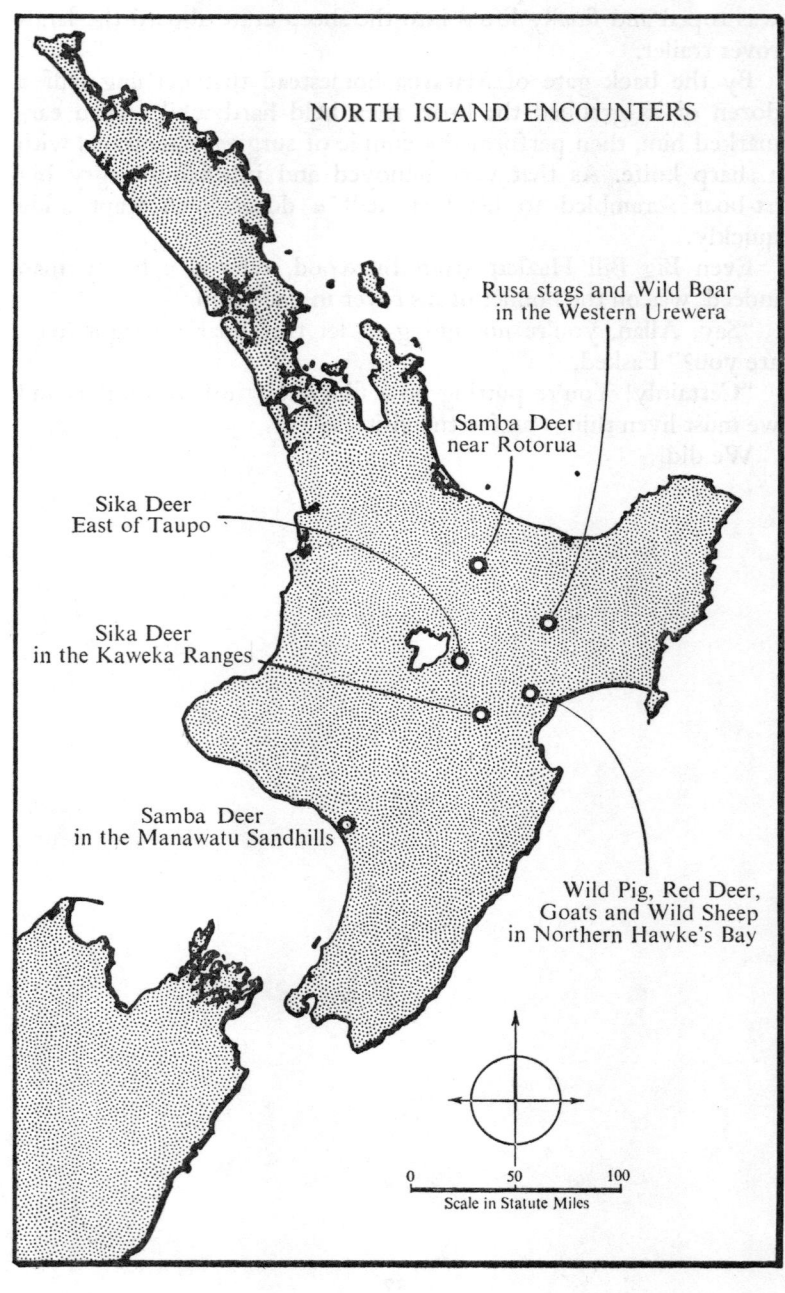

PART II
HUNTING THE NORTH ISLAND

The Rusa Roared Twice

I WAS STRUGGLING through a tangle of manuka and bracken fern when the rusa roared. Abruptly I haltered, wondering if at last I really had heard that rare and elusive note. Then the stag roared clearly again—an abrasive bellow, with none of the coughs and grunts peculiar to the red stag. It was a harsh roar, sounding from four to five hundred yards up the steep gorge ahead. I struggled to a better vantage point, and swung my binoculars to scan the gully.

My first visit to the rusa territory had been in March over four years earlier. I hadn't carried a rifle that trip as I was guiding an American, Paul Ilgenfritz from Pennsylvania.

The rusa deer are quite unlike any other deer in New Zealand. The hinds are rather tiny creatures, no bigger than a fallow doe, but with large rounded ears. Rusa deer are a drab brown all over, with no "give-away" white tail markings, so they blend perfectly with the fern and manuka. They move somewhat aimlessly in short dashes, head held low to the ground and, if undisturbed, I believe they spend all their lives within a hundred yards of one spot, for day after day I came to watch for the same solitary animal, or tiny band, feeding on their own secluded clearing or sunny slope.

Actually Paul and I had caught a fleeting glimpse of a fine stag during that first trip. Rusa hunting is an unusual business, for we were camped on the rear of a lush cow farm not a mile from the milking plant. From Rotorua or Taupo you swing east through the Kaingaroa pine plantations, sweep briefly down to the green pastures around Murupara before the highway climbs into the vast forests of the Urewera. That's where the rusa herd roams, right along the western edge of the Urewera, hiding by day in the almost impenetrable jungle of fern and scrub, grazing by night on the rich cow pastures of Galatea. The farms are flat, right up to the mountains which rear sharp and precipitous in a ragged wall, broken here and there where a river rushes down from the mountains or a tumbling mountain torrent spews shingle across the farms.

On that first visit our farmer host, George Isley, was adamant that our chances of a trophy in daylight were virtually nil, but Paul and I were on the trail before dawn, stalking the wide area of the Horomanga riverbed, dense with manuka and bracken, raupo and blackberry. Within minutes of camp, before sun-up, we saw a rusa doe and fawn sprinting across the gravel, but they were the only game we glimpsed.

That evening and again the next morning we stalked the scrub edge, skirting the dairy farms, tramping south almost three miles. We saw deer tracks and deer trails in the dew-drenched grass, and also discovered an elaborate brand new deer cullers' tent camp in the manuka. George was extremely angry with the proposed Government rusa extermination policy due to start in a few weeks, for the Galatea farmers cherish their rusa deer, claiming that after all they feed the deer, and that the rusa only hide on the edge of the Ureweras. George insisted that my American client must come spotlighting with him and try at any costs to shoot a rusa before the cullers downed them with dogs and snipers, or buckshot and night lights.

About 9.30 pm he arrived with his friend Laurie Turner, both on a small Ferguson tractor. Paul and I rode a rear-mounted platform, a heaving jolting vehicle rich with exhaust fumes. There were opossums everywhere—dozens, literally hundreds of them, all dark brown furred creatures, orange eyes glinting in the torchlight. Opossums sat on every fencepost, hung swaying in the manuka and queued to swing up the cabbage trees. The tractor forded the shallow river, bumped through bracken and blackberry. Several rusa does were seen calmly eyeing the spotlight, for the current venison campaign had hardly begun, and poaching hadn't reached its present intensity. You won't find the rusa there now—they're hanging in a freezer somewhere.

The tractor swung past a stand of tall manuka and the lights caught a huge rusa stag rushing into the scrub. That stag knew what the lights meant. The tall set of antlers were briefly outlined, long polished tops flashing briefly, then he was gone.

In 1963 I was back at Galatea again with two mates, Russell Sattrup and Viv Severinsen. This time it was spring, mid-September—an awkward time for a farmer like me, but lambing was almost over and docking could wait while I went stalking. George Isley, our Galatea friend, advised us to come then—he believed the rusa could be rutting, but they weren't. At dawn we fruitlessly stalked the scrub edge, but by day we ranged the Galatea mountain slopes, fighting the tangle of scrub which clothes the whole face. Manuka and fern intertwine ten feet high and you can't see over or under it. Struggle on to a sharp spur and we couldn't see above the scrub, though I did try climbing a spindly manuka on occasion.

Red deer smash a trail through this type of growth, but the small rusa tunnel underneath, so uphill you literally crawl and downhill you slide, feet first. In such growth the chance of a shot is nil.

We somehow climbed high to the forest 2,000 feet above, but saw little sign of rusa in the bush. Once or twice, stalking alone, we glimpsed rusa does ghosting away, but further back in the forest is the haunt of the red deer.

Exploring far into a remote watershed, descending into a rocky, forested canyon up the Ohuta, I watched a six-point red stag browsing on a cliff, but he was safe from my rifle. A rusa stag was my quarry. One evening Russell was spying from a promontory high above the river flats and saw several rusa hinds emerge in the dusk and play on a pumice knoll. Then he saw a rusa stag cross a narrow opening in the scrub, too far away.

A year later, Russell and I were back again, this time in October. We were gaining experience now, finding a few openings in the manuka, avoiding the worst scrub ridges. Russell was spending much of his time glassing from a commanding knob, waiting for a rusa stag to wander out either way below or in a dense gorge looping behind his ridge. I had found a high steep spur across the river where a handful of rusa deer lived, but never an antlered deer did I see. That trip ended abruptly with an emergency dash home due to a family sickness.

The next trip was an unscheduled visit. Lloyd Tillett, from Wyoming, turned up quite unexpectedly at my home in Hawke's

Bay so I hurriedly arranged a fallow hunt for him. Then we both headed north to stalk the sika stags. Lloyd had excellent hunting with the Japanese deer and shot three sika stags within a couple of days. I also took a lovely sika trophy, so we decided to try for a rusa too.

There had been a disastrous Urewera flood fanning out across Galatea and the Bay of Plenty a few weeks earlier, and our campsite on the Horomanga River was heaped with huge logs and debris. The river, once a haunt of excellent rainbow trout, was now buried in a welter of mud, logs and gravel which had churned down out of the Urewera.

It was raining at dawn, so Lloyd wasn't enthusiastic. A man from the desert, Lloyd almost never sees rain, and the dripping scrub didn't appeal to him. So instead of stalking the faces for rusa, we explored up the Horomanga River valley.

For some years the Forestry Department had barred all visitors while a special deer extermination experiment was attempted there. Alan Rhea, chief Wild Life officer for the project, had earlier explained the set-up—how for the previous five years five Government hunters had hunted the Horomanga, trying, with stalking and snares, spotlight and dogs, to clear out the last deer. To prevent deer infiltration from the adjacent forestry blocks these nearby areas had also been intensively hunted by other parties. Alan Rhea mentioned how hard it was to keep hunters in the Horomanga project. Deer were so scarce that the men averaged one deer per man per fortnight. Imagine stalking the endless forests day after day, perhaps shooting two deer in two days, knowing the statistics were against seeing another animal for a month. No wonder his cullers got bush-happy and once every month or so had to be carried off down to Poronui for a long weekend bombing up the sika.

Many deer must have died in the storm, having been caught in flood or avalanching hillside, for in a mile or two of riverbed we found several rotting carcasses, and one almost buried rusa stag in velvet. Since practically the last deer is supposed to have been destroyed in the Horomanga, deer causing erosion could hardly be blamed.

Wandering up the valley, taking a few pictures on the way, we came to a forestry hut with three young deer cullers in occupation. Lonely and bored with their job of firewood-splitting and track-cutting, they were delighted with company and had the billy on smartly. We yarned awhile and they said they had to spend six weeks on this job before graduating to hunting. Apart from their keep they received $34 per week; a second-rate culler got $38 and a first-class culler $40 or $42. That was in March 1964.

Lloyd and I separated and climbed the steep scrub slopes of Galatea in the evening. Neither of us saw deer and Lloyd was appalled at the hunting terrain. Next day was misty and again we saw no deer. Lloyd wasn't entranced with rusa hunting so we abandoned the stalk and went on to Rotorua to show him the thermal regions.

Russell Sattrup and I were back in Galatea during mid-winter the following July. The night I left my home storm warnings were out all over New Zealand. The desert road was under snow and the Napier-Taupo road almost closed. I threw a shovel, tow rope and wheel chains in the landrover and headed north before dawn.

Cold, chill daylight was breaking as I climbed over Titiokura Mountain, with snow dusting the road on the crest of every hill. But there was clear weather ahead and frosts at Taupo. Russell, down from the Waikato, met me at the Rainbow Mountain corner and before noon we had our tent pitched on the familiar campsite by the Horomanga River.

Deer were moving after the storm and that evening I spotted several rusa hinds either crossing a tiny opening in the dense scrub or lying dozing in the afternoon sun. Some were so distant that even after spying them with my binoculars they were quite indiscernible with the naked eye.

We had a disturbed night, for by midnight we were out with torches tying down the tent which flapped wildly in a sudden squall. By 1.30 am Russell was roaming about wanting to know the time. At 3 am he jerked me awake urgently to say he had heard a rusa roar three times, but it never roared again. At 4.30 am the full moon was rising over the Urewera as Russell leapt out of bed, bawling: "It's daylight. We're late. Get up!" I glanced at my watch and moaned. "It's only moonlight. Here's my torch and watch," and rolled over. Talk about tomcats and moreporks.

Even so Russell was up soon after 5 am and a chill breakfast was over by 6.30. It was searing cold, white frost freezing everything. My impatient mate was raring to go into the night. "You could see a rusa stag 100 yards from camp," I said. "There are deer tracks in the sand. Wait until it's nearly daylight."

But Russell was gone into the shadowy dawn. I had hardly left camp—it was still quite dark—when I heard his gunshot across the river followed by a quick dull "thomp".

"Sounds like a hit," I muttered to myself, and hurried off along the scrub edge, frost crunching underfoot. A mile to the south I stamped across a dry wash and climbed the crumbling bank. I froze still as a spike rusa, fat and round, walked on to a rise 140 yards ahead. I was following the fenceline along an opening crushed in the tall manuka. The spiker was right by the fence, ready to jump over. Gradually, very, very slowly, I eased to my heels and squatted on the frozen gravel. Then a hind, only half the size of the male, stepped from the bushes. Moving ever so slowly, I checked the scope sight to make sure there was no fogging, gently eased a shell into the breech "just in case".

The two deer stood about, then the hind disappeared briefly and re-appeared through the fence.

I was getting restless, impatient to be on my way and look more country over in that first critical hour of dawn, when I was thrilled to see antlers, great heavy tines deeply tipped with white, lifting above the rise. My .243 was centring on his chest as the magnificent rusa stag stepped on to the little spur by the fence.

"Wait a moment," I told myself. "Straight chest is a killing hit, but deer sometimes plunge away desperately before they go down." The stag carried the six points of a mature rusa, but the tines themselves were extraordinarily long and heavy in beam. The stag was almost jet black and probably weighed three times the weight of the spiker. Rusa hinds are extremely small in comparison to the males. When the stag pivoted aside, presenting his left shoulder, the scope post climbed third way up, steadied and touched off.

The gunshot boomed out, the stag leapt four feet clear of the ground and charged madly down and away. I ran forward, trying to keep track of him past a scraggy bunch of whippy manuka. A small panic-stricken rusa dashed through the manuka;

another darted along the fringe, paused, then dived for heavy scrub. I ran over the rise and surprised two more rusa does in the shelter of a spreading manuka. They plunged into the thickets.

Quite confident that a prized rusa stag was mine at last, that he had probably dashed fifty yards dead on his feet with a heart shot, I stepped down into the scattered manuka thickets and started searching.

I looked rather hurriedly at first, expecting to see the stag piled dead in every piece of cover. I then quartered the whole area thoroughly. The blood trail was sparse and petered out after forty or fifty yards, and the frozen ground showed little definite sign. Splayed hoofprints dashed into the manuka in several places, but the herd of deer had obviously grazed and played in the area all night, for there was a maze of criss-crossing deer marks.

Once I caught a movement up the mountain, glanced up at a tiny opening in the dense scrub to see six rusa deer filing across. Three were rusa hinds each with a large fawn. Then a rusa stag, only the second I had ever seen in daylight, followed, paying close attention to the females.

I believe I could have shot the stag—the range was around 300 yards—but this was a young beast and, although he carried six points, the tines themselves were short and the antler length in the main beam was not long.

For two solid hours I searched the paddock while the sun gradually climbed higher and the swirling, drifting fog faded and dispersed. Disappointed, but still convinced my trophy lay somewhere handy, I walked the mile and more back to the camp, boarded the rover and drove down to enlist the aid of George Isley, his two active sons and their dog Rusty. A genial neighbouring farmer, Theo Mills, and his employee, Laurie Turner, collected rifles and gladly joined the search. Like most dogs Rusty has a nose for deer, but though we looked and searched and poked, the stag was never located.

Russell and I were back in Galatea trophy hunting five months later, in November. Yes, trophy hunting for rusa, when almost all other deer are in velvet. The great majority of rusa stags drop their antlers towards Christmas, and are only in the hard again by June, with the rut in mid-July. Like their cousin the samba, not quite all the stags drop their antlers every year, which was the reason why Paul Ilgenfritz, the American, and I saw a fine antlered rusa back in early March on my first visit long ago. You could just possibly be fortunate enough to shoot a rusa stag with antlers in the hard at any period of the year, and the same rule applies to samba.

George, our farmer host, and his two boys greeted us with the welcome news that Russell's rusa trophy had been found. Remember Russell's impatience to leave camp before daylight and his gunshot in near darkness, just across the river. Well, he had come on a bunch of rusa deer on a raupo swamp in the manuka, and fired at the largest animal, dimly silhouetted in the scope sight. Russell didn't realise he had hit it, but I had heard the bullet strike home. We had both searched next day without success, but the rabbiter had found the rotting carcass many weeks afterwards.

Although he didn't know it until months later, my mate actually killed two rusa stags that day in mid-winter. Patiently glassing from high above, looking down into the scrub flats along the river, he saw two rusa, a stag and hind, lying down in a tiny opening in the manuka and fern. Marking the spot by a cabbage tree, he descended from his lookout hill, and stalked through the jungle scrub to within 150 yards of his quarry. Russell couldn't see them of course, so he scaled a terrace and climbed a quaking matipo tree. The doe was partly in view but the stag was still hidden, so he whistled. The stag leapt up and Russell shot quickly. My mate was dismayed to discover the stag was a one-prong freak, with only a lone antler, not even a sign of the pedicle knob on the other side! He had had the skin cured from that stag, and now he was back at Galatea, delighted with an unexpected set of six-point rusa antlers to hang on the wall.

By now we were both thoroughly familiar with the rusa territory, so as usual we parted to stalk our favourite possies, crawling up the steep spurs or sneaking into the tiny clearings. The weather this trip was wet and unpleasant and the dense scrub seemed worse.

One evening I climbed the hill across the river with Russell as the weather cleared. Looking back down to the flats far below we could see the bones of Russell's July kill bleaching in the blackberries, and an eight-point red stag in velvet, fat and rounded, feeding in a little secluded raupo swamp hidden on a fern terrace. Russell carried on to stalk the bush and spotted a rusa stag. He pulled the trigger but the rifle hung fire and he had a miss.

I waited on a knob until the shadows were low, then eased down to see into a hidden gully. A long slip scarred the other slope and while I watched, a big black boar wandered on to the clay. At first glance I knew this pig was a good one for I could see the wicked white tusks curving wide.

I carried the 30.06 this time, loaded with 150-grain silver-tip cartridges. That's a long-range bullet, with not much drop, but I estimated the range at 350 yards. I aimed at the top of the shoulder and the pig leapt down and across the slip and into the scrub.

Then a five-finger scrub shook convulsively, twenty yards in the bush, and I heard a long gasp. I figured that it was the boar's death rattle, and it was! He was a real Captain Cooker, with long tapering snout, small hips and high shoulders. Not a big pig, but a fine set of tusks. The bullet had struck low, right at the lower brisket. I skinned the pig right back to the navel as I intended an unusual mount, a half pig standing on the floor of the trophy room, emerging from a screen of fern.

That pig was certainly lousy. At midnight I was standing naked while Russell squirted me all over with bug bomb, and my clothing and sleeping bag.

We stalked the bush edge, climbed the slopes but no rusa stags were seen. On the last morning I set off round the flats and eased past two red deer hinds which galloped out across the clover fields.

Reds are very uncommon on the Galatea faces, but apparently a few appear around fawning time. I remarked to George on the way out that I had seen the hinds, and though I wouldn't have minded venison, refrained from shooting.

"That's the only reason we let you on," George retorted. "If you had shot them you wouldn't be here!"

When Russell and I swung into George Isley's home next July the weather was rough and violent, rain teeming in from the east and a wild gale screaming out of the Ureweras. George hadn't expected us, due to a poor 'phone connection, and said that two photographers more or less had sole rights in the area, and that all shooting either by private stalkers or by Government deer cullers was barred. Since Russell had only collected our hunting permits in Rotorua that morning it seemed there was some mix-up, so we wandered along to Theo Mills's home and spent the stormy afternoon yarning and drinking his coffee. The two photographers staying there were decent chaps and we enjoyed their company. Gordon Roberts, chief Wild Life officer down South Canterbury way, had taken three months' leave of absence, and was collecting material and photos for a photographic book on New Zealand wild game. His friend and opponent, tall Johnnie Johns, was employed in the same work for the Government.

Gordon, after months of patient work, was waiting for his film to be processed, confident that he had finally achieved outstanding photos of wild rusa stags in their natural habitat. Now he was helping his opponent get his pictures, a very fine gesture. Go buy their books—they should be interesting.

Gordon and Johnnie Johns weren't operating across the Horomanga; they thought they could obtain Johnnie's pictures on the slopes behind George Isley's place, so we amicably agreed to skirt each other's territory.

Russell and I set up the tent at dusk in rain and violent gusts of wind. One row of guy ropes were tied to a stout barbed wire fence, but the tent pegs shifted, so we moved Russell's Skoda car and my new landrover in as anchors. The poles still blew aside so we carried sodden logs from the river, tied heaps of them outside the walls and more inside. It was a wild night, but the rain eased towards daylight.

Russell stalked across the river, climbing high to the bush edge. He had a quiet day, glimpsing only two deer in the forest at different times. About 2 pm wild barking from a pair of dogs hunting down in the Horomanga attracted him and he came down to investigate, believing they might have a stag bailed. But the dogs kept shifting and the local farmers were doubtful, thinking they were stray dogs after opossums. I went along the bush fringe for some three miles but saw no deer. Once or twice I climbed way up into the scrub, looking for vantage posts to crane above the manuka. I came on a couple of Gordon Roberts's tracks, carefully cut so he could quietly stalk openings with his camera.

A sixteen-point fallow buck shot high on Mt Creighton near Lake Wakatipu.

On the Trail to Never Never. Wilby at a fly camp in the Harrison River Fiordland.

A billy goat trophy taken by W. Koller. Beyond Lake Wakatipu can be seen the valleys of the Greenstone and Caples.

This huge wild boar was shot on Mararoa Station in Southland.

A long gully climbs steeply into the range and I struggled up the dense spur on the northern rim. Across the gorge, three, four, five hundred yards and more distant, there was an almost vertical sheltered face, clothed in manuka and fern, toe-toe and regrowth scrub. But here and there were a few grassy openings and a couple of old slip scars. Many hours I'd spent glassing the ridge, and usually if you watched and waited long enough, a rusa would show up somewhere, lying screened in the bracken or nibbling at a succulent five-finger.

Craning over swaying manuka or peering between the branches makes glassing difficult, and long-range shooting nearly impossible, so in three vantage spots, each half a mile apart, I trimmed off a handful of manuka saplings to give myself a damp, hidden lookout. I spent seven hours on the spur until sundown, carefully studying five different rusa deer which browsed and drowsed on the distant sunny slope. Apart from one doe and fawn, all were lone hinds, for the rusa is rather a solitary creature. Never—yet, in four years—had I seen a stag on the face, but then I had hardly seen one anywhere else either.

The next morning there was a frost at daylight and light snow was frosting the rim of the forest high above. I stalked the scrub edge at first light and in one place came on two rusa does.

Towards noon I climbed again, scrambling up the same spur I had investigated the previous day. I was approaching my lowest lookout point when the rusa stag roared—a startling and thrilling sound.

After a prolonged search with the binoculars, I climbed to the next lookout and spotted two rusa does. One distant creature was grazing; the other was lying, almost invisible, beneath a toe-toe bush.

An hour later I crawled up a rusa tunnel and out to a high knob. High above the Galatea flats I glanced down toward our camp, a mile and a half distant, and instantly noted that Russell's car had been shifted. I focussed the glasses on our tent and was excited when I saw Russell had shot another rusa stag, tall antlers leaning against a post.

Wondering briefly if I was ever going to get another chance at a trophy rusa myself, I turned away and pushed through the screening bushes to my hidden hide. Swinging the big 20 X across the gorge toward the toe-toe, I was thrilled to see four or five rusa hinds lying grouped together in the warm winter sunshine. I never did count them, for roving binoculars caught the flash of ivory points. A rusa stag at last, lying dozing with his harem, beneath a small manuka bush. The stag turned his head.

"My oath, he's as big as a wapiti!" I thought to myself. "Those antlers make Johann Kalff's rusa look like a spiker!"

I reached for the 30.06 and realised my heart was pumping, hands shaking and eyes blurred. "Hell, you're getting old, Keith. That climb sure took it out of you." But it was buck fever. I was disgusted. Twenty-five years of the world's hunting trails behind me, and now buck fever like a youngster with his first stag in the sights.

I took a deep breath, turned away from the deer and purposefully and firmly relaxed. I checked the scope sight, loaded an extra cartridge into the breech and checked that I had four or five extra rounds handy.

The range was extreme, at least 350 yards, possibly 400, and there was absolutely no hope of closing the distance. The stag lay in quite dense cover—the bush below and to the left scattered manuka, with close scrub beyond. The first shot had to count.

Using a sturdy lancewood I steadied the heavy rifle, aiming an inch under the hairline atop the buck's shoulder, and squeezed the trigger gently. As the gunshot echoed across the mountain the herd split and fled. One rusa hind darted down and across a slip, and another dived headlong straight into the bush, but my attention was on the stricken stag. He leapt to his feet, flung forward past the kanuka, and stood facing me, head sagging, obviously hard hit. I flung another shot at him, but shot too hurriedly and the rusa leapt blindly forward and down into the bushes.

For ten minutes longer I crouched with the rifle, then the binoculars, searching every yard of the distant slope. Nothing moved except one puzzled hind, left behind in the panic and now not sure where to go.

Slipping the cartridge out of the breech, I angled down into the gorge and climbed steeply through the birches. As I approached the scene of action, I paused to lever a bullet back up the spout for I recalled Russell's remark that morning. "Keith, be careful if you wound a rusa. I hear they are nasty customers."

That the stag was wounded there was no doubt. Blood splayed the bushes leading down and around the mountain, deep in cover all the way. At first the trail led downwards but then swung along and up the hillside. That was a bad sign. A sore, hurt beast seldom climbs. Dismayed, wondering if I was in for another long search, I followed cautiously, rifle swinging ahead ready to stop a charge if necessary.

I edged over another rise and there was my quarry lying dead. It was a beautiful animal, in its prime, carrying the six full points.

Skinning out the headskin I was surprised at the great thickness of hide, much heavier than a red stag, though from a smaller animal. The hide on the shoulder was more like the shield on a wild boar.

I removed the antlers and cape, then boned out all the meat. Noting that the bullet had not left the body I opened the chest cavity and found the mushroom projectile had pierced through the heart and lay under the skin on the opposite shoulder. The bullet had dropped fifteen inches. That shot was a long one!

Dead on his feet, the gallant rusa had covered nearly 150 yards. Glassing into the face from the other side I had no idea how steep, almost perpendicular, the slope was or how dense the scrub. The weighty load of venison, plus rifle on one shoulder and antlers on the other, caught at every bush and branch, and several times I almost overbalanced and fell ten or fifteen feet into the bush or fern below. Sometimes I crawled, pushing the rifle ahead, dragging the antlers behind, but no thicket could damp my elation.

At last I had a rusa to be proud of. Russell's new head was also a fine trophy, very long and heavy in timber, as rusa should be. Unfortunately one brow tine had half its length broken off.

Russell had shot the animal at dawn, across the Horomanga, at the edge of the manuka by George Isley's fenceline. He had passed a stand of scrub where the stag was concealed and the rusa had panicked, leaping across the opening toward denser cover. Russell glimpsed it again and down it went to his rifle.

It was an immense beast with massive body and headskin, even heavier and thicker than my own. Though Russell's was a considerably larger animal, the skull on my trophy was slightly larger and the teeth were of an older stag.

I believe mine was a mountain stag, living hard, never venturing down to the bush flats. Russell's beast had been grazing on the rich river terraces for years—we had seen his hoof prints often. He holed up each day in a dense fern gully leading into the Ureweras, retreating unseen, unheard, further into the trees or scrub if danger threatened.

But at last the stag had lingered too long and Russell had his trophy. I have a feeling it was the same great rusa stag I had seen at night four years before on my first trip into the Galatea country with Paul Ilgenfritz.

Search for a Sika Stag

THE SIKA DEER TERRITORY lies south-east of Lake Taupo, so with a permit to hunt the beech forest of State Forest 90 in our pockets, my friend Wilby Oliver and I turned south off the Napier-Taupo highway, down across the gaunt tussock plains towards the bush. For many years post-splitters had carved at the massive birches, selling countless thousands of battens and red birch fenceposts.

The logging trail wound for eleven miles into the beech forest, but we had not travelled very far before being temporarily blocked by a bulldozer and a huge, felled beech log. We talked awhile with the post-splitters and admired the marvellous stand of red beech. Towering forty to fifty feet to the first limb and three, four, five or even more feet in diameter, each tree yielded enormous quantities of timber. Unfortunately beech, whether the red beech or its tougher cousin the black beech, is only suitable for fencing, as they carry an acid sap which corrodes nails and stains the timber. Red beech not infrequently produce the huge wart-like masses on their trunks, known as burls, which if made into furniture, feature a maze of tiny knots and whorls.

Some six miles in the bush is the post-splitters' permanent camp, a sagging array of dingy huts, and just short of there we saw our first sika deer. Heavy regrowth of beech and wineberry had choked an ancient logging area, and as the V8 spun around a tight turn two deer scampered down the trail. Sika deer aren't very large, perhaps half the size of a red deer, and are often lightly spotted all their lives. Instead of the sharp tipped ears of a red, the sika deer ears are quite rounded, and they sport a very prominent white tail. I tramped hard on the brakes, skidding the truck, not wishing to kill my first sika deer under the bonnet, and the two deer leapt into the bushes.

Quite reasonably all shooting is barred until past a stiff little ridge beyond the camp. Wilby and I cruised the old trail until it faded out into half a dozen overgrown tracks, then searched about for a campsite. Pleasant dry sites for a tent were not hard to find, but water was a problem in the porous pumice plateau, many of the valleys being quite dry.

The weather looked promising, so we didn't trouble to erect a tent. Instead we slung a green tarpaulin between a couple of birches.

We tramped south down a muddy dozer trail, stepping lightly through the pleasant forest. The little valley closed in, the trail turned sharply and as we bent to crawl under a grove of twisted and gnarled old fuchsia trees, there was a sharp snap as a twig cracked, the whisper of parted leaves, and a pair of sika darted away. Sika deer have a distinct preference for these little fuchsia hollows.

After a mile or so the bulldozer trail disappeared completely but we pushed on until the trees changed character, becoming smaller with more pepperwood undergrowth. Swinging right to make an exploratory circuit back to camp, we discovered a pleasant forest stream, gurgling through green moss-encrusted boulders. Though we weren't familiar with either map or territory, we decided that this was probably the Hinemaia, which drains into Lake Taupo. The big forested basin of State Forest 90 is the easiest place to get lost in I know of. Low rolling hills, completely clothed in dense birch bush, sprawl haphazardly, and the few streams wander casually through the sombre forest, either swelling Taupo in the west or joining the turbulent Mohaka far to the south-east.

My mate and I were stepping quietly through the bush, figuring our camp was somewhere not far ahead, when we came on a compass arrow scraped in the damp earth. North and south were clearly indicated.

The sun had disappeared in a light drizzle. I studied the drawn compass, muttering to Wilby, "Do you think north lies up that arrow?"

We both felt that our truck and camp were just over the hill ahead, but the compass sign had unsettled us, so we decided to swing hard right and cut our back trail. This we did, and camp *was* just where we had figured. I reached into the truck, and pulled out the compass I should have been carrying. North was a few degrees off to the left of where we had dead reckoned, though we had completed a forest circuit of some three miles and walked straight back to our camp.

The sika bucks should have been rutting, but we had heard no whistles, so toward dark we cruised the forest road for a few miles, occasionally stopping to listen. I swung hard on the steering, wheeling right and left where the trail wove between piled heaps of discarded rotting logs, then skidded to a halt as I glimpsed a great dark sika stag standing watching us, shadowed in the tree. He carried a lovely set of antlers, wide and very long, four points to a side. Even before the V8 had halted the stag turned and sprang lightly away, bending his head to avoid the branches. My mate and I spread and followed but saw the stag no more. The buck had been pawing out a stump in the peculiar manner which the rutting sika deer have of proclaiming their exclusive territory.

Early that evening Wilby and I wriggled into our sleeping bags, for we had been driving much of the previous night, but at about 11 pm car lights swung on to our camp and the first load of Auckland hunters, down for the weekend, spilled from their vehicle. They had finished work at 5 pm, driven for five or six hours, and after a few hours' sleep would be out hunting at daylight on Saturday morning.

While they pitched an igloo tent by carlight, we brewed them a cup of tea. The whole company had just settled into bed again when the next vehicle came grinding down the pumice trail, sending its light into our tents. That party reversed and camped a mile back up the road, but every hour until morning new carloads of hunters arrived and either set up camp or just noisily discussed the situation and departed. By Saturday dawn, as I reached for the kerosene to fill our little primus cooker, there were five new parties of eager hunters parked and camped close by.

The torch was feeble and I spilled a little fuel over the primus and on to the ground. Wilby knelt to ignite the meths. and a thin tongue of flame crept down the outside of the fuel tank and licked the spilt kerosene on the dry soil. I turned away, picked up the billy and went down to the creek. As I came back past the big birch there was a vivid scarlet burst of flame within our tent and a muffled explosion. Wilby yelled, burst toward me, and I was appalled to see he was aflame, his shirt, hands, face and hair all alight. I grabbed him as he staggered blindly past and smothered the flames, I don't know how. Then the chaps from the next tent were rushing to help, kicking the blazing battered remnant of the exploded primus from the tent, desperately grabbing parka or pullover to beat at the splashed flames licking at the green tarpaulin fly. Wherever the exploding kerosene had landed on the ground, our foodstuff, sleeping bags, all were on fire.

We stamped the last flames into the dirt then had a look at Wilby. The skin on hands and forehead was peeling in irregular wrinkled splotches. I had some burn ointment handy, laid it on gently, then hurried him into the V8 and we charged through the silent bush, where the night's shadows still persisted. In Taupo, forty miles away, we searched out a doctor from his breakfast, and had Wilby's burns treated and bandaged. Then, the hunt abandoned, we drove back to roll up the scorched tent fly and retrieve our gear. Several of the stalkers were in from their morning hunt and some of them had seen deer. One boy from Putaruru had shot a small six-point sika stag. Another group were bow hunters, including the national secretary of their organisation. Just before we left one chastened bow hunter walked very quietly into camp, sat silent for quite a period before confessing that he had been completely and utterly lost for some hours, and had stumbled on to a logging trail completely by chance.

It was noon as we farewelled the returning stalkers and set out sadly for Hawke's Bay.

My second trip to the sika territory was an entirely different venture.

Paul Ilgenfritz, my guest from Pennsylvania, had arrived in Auckland on the *Mariposa*. I met him with the landrover, and by nightfall he had his first New Zealand trophies, three fine billy goats. Next day Paul stalked the goats again, before we headed for Rotorua to hunt small wallaby of the region, to startle a couple of red deer, and to use up a considerable amount of Paul's 16 mm movie film on Rotorua's trout pools and geysers. Near Galatea, at the edge of the Urewera, Paul secured a rusa stag, probably the first ever taken in New Zealand by an American.

Paul had mentioned that two acquaintances of his, hunters from his home city of York, in Pennsylvania, were in New Zealand on safari with guide Rex Forrester, and he wondered what trophies they had shot. With New Zealand's criss-cross of roads and maze of mountains the chances of a casual meeting must have been a million to one. Paul was filming the geothermal bores of Wairakei when I glimpsed Rex Forrester's safari waggon through the steam and flagged him down.

Rex, in his neat khaki drills, was his usual alert self but his two American hunters, Paul Ilgenfritz's friends, were haggard and unshaven. They were delighted with their New Zealand trip. They had enjoyed their thar and chamois stalking on Godley Peaks so much that they had extended the hunt by several days. They had shot excellent fallow deer too, but Paul was quick to display his own goat horns, better trophies than those shot by both his friends. Bill Consley, one of the Americans, does a considerable amount of writing for American hunting magazines and also lectures extensively, and when Rex had finally corralled his hunters again and they had gone, Paul wryly remarked: "Bill Consley tells a story so well that if a mouse crosses the track he makes it sound like he was charged by a bull elephant."

Paul Ilgenfritz was a very agreeable chap, small and lightly built, always nattily dressed, a non-smoker and non-drinker. He had hunted extensively in Alaska on numerous occasions with my frontier friend Johnny Luster and had shot a huge brown bear on Kodiak Island as it stalked and charged Paul and his guide. Paul carried a 30.06 Remington rifle, with Weaver scope. On snap shots Paul was accurate and he was absolutely deadly on running game, but on the easy deliberate shot, he missed more than he should have done, for the rather heavy 30.06 recoil made him flinch and pull off-target.

I snaked the rover down the bush trail through State Forest 90, passed through the familiar camp and braked hard as I met two stalkers round a sharp bend in the wineberry. They were Jack Dillon and a cobber from Taupo coming in from a day's stalking.

Near a pleasant stream a couple of miles short of the trail's end, Paul gave me a hand to set up camp. It was a considerably more elaborate affair than my last sika camp, with a large airy 10 x 14 tent, a couple of safari stretcher beds, even a folding table and a pair of chairs.

One unpleasant aspect of the beech forest on Paul's hunt was the activity of opossum hunters. The whole bush stank of dead and rotting opossums and there was a pile of skinned carcasses every few yards.

Towards dark Paul and I walked up a forest ridge, and circled back to the trail. We saw no deer, though we did startle a red deer hind. She dashed through the bushes, then barked loudly half a dozen times from the next spur.

At daylight the next morning we hunted westwards, climbing an old bulldozer track to a low, flat-topped hill. The trail wandered haphazardly through the trees and suddenly two red deer hinds charged past us. The hillside became more precipitous, and finally we found ourselves on a cliff point high above a huge forested valley. Seven or eight hundred feet below the Hinemaia Stream plunged over a waterfall into a basin. We retraced our steps for half a mile, scrambled down across the Hinemaia, climbed silently up through the tall, silent trees. Near the stream the bush was quite open, but the beech forest varied considerably in stalking visibility, some areas being choked with dense pepper-wood undergrowth.

Paul Ilgenfritz remarked on the lovely serenity and silence of our New Zealand forests, with no red-coated hunters or sound of gunshots every few minutes. In Paul's small home state of Pennsylvania there is a two-week deer hunting period each fall when almost a million hunters all take to the woods together with a licence for one buck deer each. Approximately 80,000 deer are killed, a chance of only one in twelve that you will bring home venison. On the eve of deer opening, Paul stated it was necessary to reach your hunting area by midnight to get car parking on the side of the country road, and that if you could travel 100 yards in any direction in the woods without meeting another hunter, then you certainly had the territory to yourself.

A native pigeon floated down to perch above our heads. The American reached for his movie, delighted with the lovely bird, for Paul was a keen ornithologist and member of several bird societies.

The birches closed in, becoming denser along a little stream. We tensed, Paul's rifle ready as we spied movement in the bushes, then a red deer fawn and its mother browsed into view. Though only forty or fifty yards away, the deer didn't detect us and we enjoyed watching them as they moved slowly away.

Later in the afternoon, we cruised down the winding forest road, weaving through the trees, dipping into gullies and hollows. We walked up a logging trail, and plunged into bush until a dense stand of pepperwood forced us to detour down a low ridge.

A sika stag stood in an opening beneath a huge red birch. As Paul's rifle steadied on its target I felt myself tense, desperately hoping he would shoot straight, for this would probably be his only chance.

The American fired and a moment later my own gunshot blended and echoed with his. Paul had hit his stag vitally. Perhaps I shouldn't have shot but I wasn't taking any chances.

Paul was elated with his sika stag, so early next day we dismantled the tent and turned southwards.

Hunting roles were reversed on my next sika hunt. Instead of being guide, I was doing the hunting with an experienced young stalker from Taupo leading the way.

With my wife and three youngsters I had been on holiday to Rotorua and returning through Taupo, Jack Dillon had invited me to speak and show my Alaskan slides to the Taupo Deerstalkers' Association. "Bring your boots and rifle," the letter stated. "I'll arrange a sika hunt for you."

When young Bruce Sowersby swung his vehicle into the motel to pick me up a couple of hours before dawn, heavy frost dusted Taupo. A hungry opossum or occasional gawky hare were the only life on the frozen tarseal as we roared through the star-studded night.

At daybreak Bruce swung his truck off the trail, hid it in a nest of brush, then we loaded our rifles and climbed a faint trail through the birches. A stag with wide heavy hoofprints had passed by recently, crushing the icicles under foot as he wandered.

Bruce was climbing from a stiff little gully when I saw his rifle spring up, aim, then he scrambled up the bank and raced along the path. My companion had almost stepped on to the stag, but the big beast leapt down the track before Bruce could shoot.

"A big red stag, about ten points, and we lost him only a quarter-mile from the truck," groaned Bruce.

High on the mountain ridge we heard the high-pitched whistle of a distant rutting sika and some time later, miles away, a gunshot sounded flat and thin.

Pungent pepperwood brush crowded the higher slopes, but it didn't invade the sheltered hollows where the deciduous fuchsias flourished. Here and there Bruce pointed out the places and spun the stories of his different sika trophies shot along the range. Toward noon we drifted down a spur, which flattened to a broad shoulder before plunging steeply to the forested valley.

A flash of white rump, a screech of alarm and a sika doe went skittering through the trees.

We descended to the valley, following the rim of the gorge downstream and watching carefully, as some distance ahead we had heard the alarm whistle of a sika.

I glanced up through the trees, and spotted a handsome sika buck nibbling among the luxuriant growth. When I fired the stag sprang ahead, spun, and charged straight downhill in a mad panic-stricken rush. I fired again as he leapt a log above me, slammed another cartridge into the breech and shot a third time as the stag flashed through the trees ahead and pitched dead. Bruce had also fired once as the buck leapt blindly downhill. My first bullet had hit near the top of the shoulder, much higher than where I had aimed.

Though the buck carried six points, it wasn't a large set of antlers, and the stag was very thin due to an old suppurating wound in the right shoulder, so we hastily discarded the meat.

Sika are curious little creatures and sometimes unusual sounds, such as gunshots or people talking, draw them like a magnet. Chirping their curious alarm call, we could hear some approaching up the valley. Cautiously we fossicked through the beeches, but they were much closer than expected. A moment later a sika deer went bouncing up the far bank of the gorge and paused in some dense scrub birches. I fired. The deer disappeared and two more sika scrambled up the spur. Again a gunshot boomed through the forest and one of the two deer went rolling into the bushes by the stream. But when we descended to find it the animal was gone, leaving only a smear of blood and scattering of hoofprints. For an hour, perhaps longer, we tracked the deer along the creek, round a deer trail up to the ridge, through stands of pepperwood and beech, fuchsia and tangled lawyer, until we finally lost it completely. I doubt if the deer had been badly wounded, only creased and stunned.

I had a somewhat similar experience once in the remote forested Makarora Valley in the hinterland of Wakarara. It was the rutting season, and when I gave a bellow, a stag answered my challenge, and came charging furiously down through the trees. The beast, suddenly suspicious, halted about thirty yards away where I couldn't see him, so I cautiously climbed atop a huge red birch log. The red stag glimpsed movement through the trees, flung his great antlered head about to glare my way. I could see part of the beast's swollen neck, but a small tree hid half the stag's face. Aiming at the neck, I fired once and the stag collapsed. I walked over to the motionless beast, glanced at the long nine-point set of antlers, laid pack and rifle aside and reached for my skinning knife. Just then another deer gave a warning bark, bounced into the shadows and halted. I retrieved my .303 and gave unsuccessful chase. I wasn't gone more than five minutes, but when I returned to skin the big nine-pointer, the stag had utterly vanished, leaving only a single blood spot alongside my lonely pack. I know what had happened. The bullet merely creased the top of the stag's neck, stunning him for a short time.

I believe something similar happened to the sika doe, for when I checked the .303 on target the other day it was way off-centre, hitting more than a foot high and left. For years I hadn't used that rifle, merely carried it as a spare firearm strapped in the landrover rifle rack. Carelessly I hadn't taken the opportunity to test-shoot the rifle again before going stalking, and hence the unsatisfactory result, lost or wounded animals.

Bruce and I tramped miles down the valley, made a wide circuit through the bush without seeing any more deer and late in the evening hunted back to the truck.

A year later I soft-footed along the forest edge, hugging the shadow of the sombre trees. A mile from camp I stepped over a rise and glimpsed a fine eight-point sika buck walking purposefully ahead, just disappearing into some thin manuka. I ran after him and scrambled atop a fallen log, but the scrub screened my quarry completely. Afraid the buck might already be in the birches, I jumped from the log and crouched to scan a narrow gap between scrub and trees. A long moment, then the sika stag, suspicious and alert, stepped partly into view, outlined through a fire-scorched manuka bush. Knowing my new .243 rifle's light bullet wasn't constructed for scrub bashing I hesitated but realising another step would hide the stag for ever, I fired.

The stag spun round and dashed madly across a small clearing, disappearing into a hollow. Convinced I had shot the stag in the chest and that this was merely a desperate death run, I straddled the log again, confident, but with rifle still at the ready.

The top of the stag's long antlers came into view as the stag galloped past down a dry wash and disappeared, re-appearing far out across the plain. I flung a despairing shot at the buck and ran after him as he dipped over the hill. There was a gully not far ahead, its bed dotted liberally with scattered tanekaha bushes and matipo. Gasping, I rushed to the edge and trained my rifle on the far slope. But the stag never re-appeared and later I traced his hoofprints, splayed wide in the soft pumice soil, down into the gorge, then sharp right toward the forest, slipping from tree to tree, in cover every step of the way. There was no sign of blood.

My fourth trip after the sika deer had begun the previous day when Russell Sattrup had met me at the Rangitaiki Hotel on the Napier-Taupo highway. Russell heaved his gear in my landrover, then we lurched back through the stunted manuka, hurriedly sorted our supplies, then hitched on our rifles and packs and tramped in a few miles further under a blazing sun.

The same evening my companion and I hunted a high forested mountain together, but the heavy pepperwood undergrowth limited visibility to a yard or two. I did see one little sika doe, with big white rump patch, darting through the bushes but the chances of stumbling on a trophy buck and then getting a shot seemed remote indeed.

At daylight Russell, always a keen bush stalker, was gliding into the forest again but instead I slipped along the edge of the timber, and soon shot at the trophy sika stag as already described.

Thoroughly disappointed and somewhat puzzled I examined

my new firearm again—a dandy little .243 carbine generously presented to me by my departing American guest Bill Koller. Fitted with a spare Pecar vari-power 3-7 X scope, I had sighted the new rifle in quickly and roughly the day before my trip, well enough to knock a six-inch chunk of 4 x 2 pine across the next hill every shot at 200 yards.

The .243 is an extremely light and accurate rifle, sending a deadly 100-grain bullet zipping along at over 3,070 feet per second. For comparison, the faithful old .303 trundles a 174-grain projectile through the ether at around 2,400 feet per second. While the .243 has an exceptionally flat trajectory, the lightly constructed bullet mushrooms instantly, and sometimes disintegrates when deflected with scrub or twig. On the other hand, aiming at a running stag through the Prewera bush, I have put a .303 bullet right through a solid green six-inch birch tree and still brought down a red stag on the far side.

Wondering with disgust if my bullet had deflected on a twig, or if I had just missed an easy shot, I tramped disconsolately along the bush edge, then turned into the birches and climbed through the mist-drenched forest on a wide circuit back to our camp. It was a cold bleak day, not very pleasant in the wet bush, but I covered a good many miles in the next six or eight hours, tramping along the main divide, drifting soundlessly into each open fuchsia hollow.

In May, the sika rut was barely over, and in fact I expected to hear a late stag whistling his challenge, for on five or six occasions I found new "stamps" freshly pawed. During the mating season, the sika buck lays claim to an area of forest and patrols a circuit of some hundreds of yards. Around the perimeter of his territory he horns and tramps out half a dozen "stamps" and visits them irregularly, checking to see if another buck is invading his domain. Pushing through dense undergrowth, I came on fresh sika deer droppings and new "stamps" or else small dainty hoof marks indicating a little group of deer in the vicinity. But a swirling indefinite breath of air probably warned the deer of my approach, even if they didn't hear me.

Pepperwoods, eight or ten feet high and laced with thorny lawyer vine, clogged the forest, straddling the concealed decaying birch logs. On hands and knees I crawled through tunnels in the undergrowth, or carefully tight-walked along ancient slippery birch logs. Even the main ridge was little clearer, except for occasional hollows, dominated by gnarled, sprawling old man fuchsia trees.

Though I saw fresh deer signs quite frequently, only one startled sika did I glimpse. I had paused to examine a new "stamp" and the deer must have been close by for I heard a twig crack. A little further down the valley the deer ran on to a rise ahead, paused briefly and was gone. Whether buck or doe I know not, though a sika it certainly was by the prominent white tail which flashed as it darted away.

A curious fact was the complete absence of red deer, though a few miles away reds were quite common.

Russell came in late that evening, delighted with a pretty eight-point sika trophy he had shot in the forest while sidling a high ridge south of the camp. Russell had looked down through the trees, had seen the buck half-hidden in the bushes and fired.

Torrential rain was falling at daylight but we still made preparations for an early start. It was as well we did for the rain eased quite swiftly and later cleared.

I stalked the forest rim again and came on a sika doe watching me curiously, wide round ears aquiver. I eased the rifle from my shoulder, slid a cartridge into the chamber, aimed without firing then said clearly: "You're dead."

Not playing her part the doe darted into the trees, a pleasant little incident. Some miles farther north I glimpsed a movement in a clearing way ahead in the manuka. I focussed the powerful 20 X binoculars, saw two deer, red or sika, so walked quietly closer to investigate. Four hundred yards away I saw the deer again—they were both sika, one a doe, the other a spike buck.

Hoping there might be a trophy buck somewhere handy I stalked closer, drifting stealthily from manuka to tussock, when two sika deer dashed into the edge of heavy scrub some 250 yards to my right. One was a spiker, the other a wide-antlered buck. A vagrant breeze must have warned them, I thought. The stag re-appeared briefly trotting across a tiny opening. My rifle sprang up, followed and touched off as he disappeared. Like the previous day I was confident of a well-aimed shot and again I was wrong for the stag suddenly came rushing down a little damp hollow straight toward me, then halted on the edge of a small gully. Again the .243 spoke but this time the buck collapsed.

The stag was a beauty, with a very wide heavy set of antlers carrying the eight points of a mature sika. I skinned out the headskin, sliced off all the meat from the fat around the little body and, loaded with antlers and venison, I tramped happily toward camp.

A long search for a sika stag was over!

Deer of the Kawekas

MY FIRST TRIP to hunt the sika deer of Hawke's Bay was in May 1967. A genial visitor, Doc Smith from Florida, and his little blonde wife Ada had been on a hunting trip in the outback of Australia and on their way back to the States they decided to stop off in New Zealand. Doc was a very keen hunter—Africa, India, Alaska, and a New Zealand trip a few years earlier.

He had missed out collecting a sika stag on his earlier New Zealand safari so I tossed equipment and tent aboard the rover and set out for the north. There was a third hunter with us, tall Barry Mabin, a neighbour from down the road. Barry had lost an argument with a tractor a few months before and was still swinging a crushed foot.

The Kawekas aren't a particularly large range, but they are surrounded by a maze of sprawling manuka-clad foothills. Sika deer have infiltrated through the Kawekas from the Kaimanawas to the north-west and the manuka brush country seems to suit these little deer.

We turned off the winding country road a few miles beyond Puketitiri at Glencoe Station. Ralf Sutton, the manager, greeted us and suggested we pitch the tent down by a shallow stream. Rich improved pastures, recently retrieved from manuka, bounded the creek, but immediately beyond the flats the tea-tree crowded the ridges. A bulldozed track wound three miles back into the scrub, climbing the wind-lashed mountain to a stand of red beech.

A wild boar at bay, surrounded by excited dogs.

The men of Mararoa Station roped the wild boar.
Left: Joe and Ron, shepherds. *Right*: Allan Bradley, owner of the station. A moment later the boar charged again, running between Ron's legs.

Victim of the storm Lloyd Tillett inspects the half-buried remains of rusa stag.

Rusa stags are exceedingly wary. To shoot two in one day was a rare treat.

Very early next morning I pointed the rover up the trail, stopping just short of a likely clearing. Fire had swept the spur clean of heavy scrub and a vigorous clover growth was losing its battle with strong, young regrowth manuka. We watched a red hind, well down into the gorge, and further on a pretty sika doe bounded away.

The main ridge was heavily clothed in dense manuka, the only breaks being wind-eroded yellow patches of dirt on the exposed western face. There seemed little chance of sighting game there, though half a mile away on a fern spur we watched a well-grown six-point red stag wandering down toward the Makaku. Once or twice we heard the peculiar grunt of a distant rutting sika stag.

We spent a pleasant morning exploring the range and glassing the surrounding mountains. Away north, green fingers of pasture marked the Pakatutu Government Development Block and somewhat closer another emerald oasis of lush grass had been carved from the scrub. It was a hot day, so during the afternoon we drove out that way and spoke to Jack Nicholas who owns the farm. We yarned awhile with him and drove on down the pumice track toward the hot springs. The trail was in poor condition; bog holes in the road had been corduroyed with bundles of manuka brush, and further on rain had gouged ruts two and three feet deep in the wheel-tracks. Straddling the ruts makes interesting driving but hard digging when the gravel collapsed and the axle grounded.

Deer sign was quite plentiful on Nicholas's young grass, but though we watched and stalked patiently into the dusk no deer were seen. They're cunning little devils, the sika, and feed out only after dark.

I was lighting the meths. stove before daylight next morning and rather carelessly let some fluid spill down the box to the ground. A mighty sheet of flame leapt over the stove and up the tent as I hurled the burner outside. Barry and Doc awoke and clawed out their sleeping bags in a couple of bounds. Setting the tent alight certainly gets your mates out of bed in the morning!

Again I eased the rover to a halt just short of a spur. While Doc Smith and Barry watched the steep valley beyond, I walked down the spur but swung about suddenly as Barry's .308 cracked once.

Three hundred yards below, Barry had sighted a sika stag, right down in the gorge, crossing a tiny opening.

"Shoot him, Doc," breathed Barry.

"Can't see him. You take the shot," answered the American.

I scrambled down through the burnt sticks and was delighted to find a fine eight-point stag lying dead in the gully. I skinned out the headskin, filled the pack with meat, and laboured back.

We saw no more deer that day, though late in the dusk we stalked a high fern ridge on Dineen's neighbouring block.

For the third and last morning I revved the rover up the bull-dozed logging track. On the summit Barry carried on with the vehicle to search to the end of the track but Doc and I headed south along the main ridge. Fierce wind had carved the soft pumice soil into hummocks and stark knobs along the crest.

I was looking rather intensely down into the eastern scrub when I heard Doc's gasp: "Keith, quick! Shoot!"

I glanced around. Three sika were bounding wildly over the ridge 100 yards ahead. As the .243 came swinging up, the leading two deer had already darted behind an eroded column of soil. The last doe was disappearing as the rifle cracked. She came sliding steeply, limply downhill. I rushed over the top. The other two deer were charging down a gravel slide. The little rifle cracked again and one flipped end over end. I shot a third time as the last deer bounded for the scrub and it too went floundering.

"Good shooting, Keith. Never seen anything like it."

"Why didn't you shoot, Doc?"

"Well, guess the action was all too quick for me. Don't believe I even cranked a shell into the breech before the last deer was dead."

The three beautiful sika skins were all expertly cured and one went to America. A couple of heavy packloads of venison brought all the meat out; then the tent came down and we headed home.

A year later the rover was climbing the road beyond Patoka and Puketitiri again. I had answered an advertisement for a sheep dog from John Strawbridge of Pakatutu and arranged to collect the animal during the May school holidays so my eleven-year-old son, Lex, could come too.

A keen young settler on a Government development block, last farm on the road, John waved us up his track.

"There are deer scattered all over," he said. "And there is a hut hidden in the bush. Belongs to some Feilding chaps, but you can use it."

The Pakatutu block is a high plateau lying between the deep manuka gorges of the Repia and Mohaka Rivers. Steep scrub gullies finger deep into John's farm, cutting the place into many long, irregular paddocks, and providing safe cover for marauding wild pigs and deer.

Driving up the farm which sprawls some three miles back, Lex and I sighted two red deer way down on a distant point. The hind had leapt the new barbed wire fence and was cropping clover, but her smaller six-month fawn was pacing impatiently up and down in the scrub. It was 2 pm on a warm afternoon and it is unusual these days to find deer in sight at that time.

Lex and I found the hut, a comfortable and extremely well-appointed structure, and towards evening explored an old logging trail out to a clearing. Part of a narrow manuka strip which had been bulldozed but never grassed and fenced, was already high in six-foot tea-tree.

Two sika does jumped through the scrub and the .243 brought one down. Way out on the grass flats a young sika stag flung up his head then ran toward us, swinging uncertainly toward the bush boundary fence.

"Come on, Lex."

We hurried down through the concealing bushes and paused as the Japanese stag came prancing round the fence corner. He was a long 200 yards away, poised unsure, directly facing our way.

The deer was a tiny narrow target for the .243 but the animal collapsed as the 100-grain projectile hit dead true.

Lex had a wide grin as we hurried down to examine our kill. A dozen times the children and I had hunted the Ruahines together and it had always been the same old story, never a deer in sight when the youngsters were along.

Night's dark shadows still touched the trees as Lex and I hurried through the bush next morning. An animal, probably a deer, smashed away through undergrowth. Way out on the fields the binoculars picked up a big dark sika stag. My son and I hurried down a concealing hollow but were still half a mile from the deer when a variable breeze drifted down the valley behind.

"Don't like that wind, Dad," announced Lex.

I didn't either. The stag had gone as Lex and I stalked on down the narrow tongue of grass towards the Mohaka. In the scrub just over the boundary fence a sika doe gazed our way, and from the trig station Lex and I sighted a pair of red hinds warming in the sun.

We left them in peace, climbed leisurely back to the rover, and drove back through farm and road down to the Mohaka. Lex had a licence to fish and the Mohaka was one of the few streams open during the bird-shooting season. One large fish promptly broke the lead and escaped with the attached wet fly, but that was the only real touch we had. We saw a large covey of quail in the Mohaka and a handsome cock pheasant flew clumsily away.

Toward dark, a cold, unpleasant breeze was bringing up rain, and we saw no deer during our evening stalk. There are wild pigs in the Pakatutu country but they must be a frustrated bunch. John Strawbridge's new fences are so well constructed that the pigs churn the soil all along the boundary line but can't get through.

Back at camp, Lex and I were cooking tea when a carnivorous opossum attacked our venison. Lex held the torch while I grabbed its tail and ejected it.

It was a squally blustery dawn as we threw the gear aboard the rover. An electrical fault caused brief dismay when the starter wouldn't turn the cold motor, so I found the crank handle. Lex pressed a small foot hard on the accelerator and the motor fired. Neither deer nor wild pig were in sight until I dipped the rover through a sunny bush hollow. A swift shot brought down a large sika doe. The deer's jaw and face were badly disfigured, possibly by a bullet, more probably by a fall long ago. All the scars had healed and the deer was extremely fat.

We had intended looking for pig down a sheltered fern face toward the Repia, but an early party of pighunters thwarted that plan.

Yes. I did remember to pick up the dog I had bought from John as we pointed the rover for home.

Sheep Hunt in Shangri-la

SHANGRI-LA is a mythical lost Eden in a forgotten valley, hidden in the mountains.

There is an abandoned valley like Shangri-la, up between Napier and Wairoa, way back against the Urewera forests. Wild pigs, goats and red deer roam the hills, but the game we were after was a trophy sheep, a wild Merino bred from the flocks abandoned long ago in 1938.

Dave Larsen had been inspecting my trophy room and remarked that I had no wild New Zealand ram horns hanging on the wall. I had never stalked wild sheep in this country and eagerly accepted his offer of a hunting trip into "Shangri-la" a few weeks later.

The first day Dave and I stalked the forgotten scrubland bordering the Mohaka at the rear of Waitere Station. The station was being broken in by the Lands and Survey Department for future settlement. Ted Theobald was the manager then and he invited us to camp in the shearers' quarters. Waitere is a remote block, over the high range beyond Tutira in northern Hawke's Bay.

We left at daybreak, tramping down an old bulldozed trail through scattered bush and tall kanuka. We saw one fresh hoofmark of deer on the track but it was the only sign we saw all day. Pigs had rooted the tough brown-top grass and as we descended the steep trail we could see across a broad sunny terrace rimmed by a steep fall into the winding Mohaka 1,000 feet below.

Cattle had been turned in to forage through the winter among the manuka thickets and occasional bands of goats scrambled the steeper bluffs. We soon sighted wild pigs, two black ones and a blue boar, rooting on a very steep bluff above the Mohaka. They were a mile away so we circled wide, and were just creeping over the bluff when six or eight goats of various hues filed out of the bushes close ahead. We quietly attempted to circle them but with the whole plateau to choose from the band of goats had to dive over the bank down among the wild pigs.

The pigs departed into cover—where we didn't know—but Dave and I prowled the flat-topped bluff with ready rifles. There was a sheltered hollow angling back from the steep scrub slope, so after a fruitless search I leaned the 30.06 against a handy sapling, and was settled comfortably when a blue boar appeared, marching through the bushes across the hollow. Quietly I reached for my weapon. The rifle spoke once and the boar pitched into the manuka.

The pig was well-grown and prime but not a particularly large specimen. We salvaged all the pork, hung it up in one of Dave's pillow cases in a shady tree, then tramped on. Goats infest this region and we could have counted a hundred on the papa cliff slope crumbling to the river far below. Away beyond, a dozen wild sheep drowsed on a sunny knob. There were two rams, which didn't appear to carry trophy heads, but just to make sure we swung aside and crept out to gaze down on them. Those sheep were as crafty as deer; they spotted us instantly and fled.

Dave had previously shot a fine Merino on a steep grass slope at the rear of a high bluff embraced by a loop of the turbulent Mohaka. Slowly and carefully we descended, angling and criss-crossing through the stands of scrub.

Half a dozen wild sheep appeared quite close, grazing in dense kanuka, and a large-horned ancient wandered over the knob. Quietly we withdrew and hurried over the crest. The ram, a big one, had already crossed a steep wash and was disappearing in semi-open scattered bushes. We could see heavy, wide horns, but how much curl there was we couldn't tell. Tensely we watched, reluctant to shoot anything but an outstanding trophy. The ram wandered briefly on to a tiny knoll, swung his head and we glimpsed a fine curl. My rifle swung up, fired as he stepped from view. Missed!

Sheep, previously unseen, darted through the manuka, bunched unseen somewhere below my target. A scraggy one trotted over the little opening on the knoll, fleeing for denser cover, and a ram, horns flung wide, followed.

"There he is!"

I shot again and the ram pivoted and collapsed downhill. Another ram, the big one, darted over the rise. I'd killed the wrong ram.

The following morning Dave and I decided to ford the broad Mohaka River and tramp in to Shangri-la. Ted suggested we double across on placid old Dolly, the packhorse, to save getting soaked.

There must have been a 20-degree frost in the river valley as Dave led the old mare up to the river and Dolly was anything but enthusiastic about breasting the mighty Mohaka that frosty July morning. We had a bridle on the horse but no saddle, merely intending to ford the river with the help of Dolly, then leave her tethered until our return. Dave is a powerfully built young chap, weighing about sixteen stone. I only clock ten and a half stone, but the two of us astride Dolly really weighed her down. It was just as well we did weigh so much, or the horse would have floated down the rapids. The Mohaka, slightly discoloured and carrying quite a fresh, surged in a broad swift flood, but didn't look really deep. We finally coaxed Dolly in and before we fully realised the extent of the flood, our horse was belly deep and then the river was surging up and over the wallowing horse.

Realising there was every chance of being swept off and drowned I shouted to Dave, "If Dolly goes down the river you hang on to her mane. I'll grab her tail and swim."

If I could, that was. We both had a rifle and frame packs strapped across our shoulders. Down went the mare, blowing bubbles like a skindiver as she submerged. The water came up to our waists but somehow we made it, and the brave old horse scrambled up the other bank. We tied her up, checked our rifles and gear, and tramped towards a large hidden valley, walled by a spectacular range of granite mountains rearing to the east. A hundred years before Te Kooti had built a fighting pa on these pinnacles.

Two deer, a hind and her yearling fawn, darted across the rocky outcrop across the manuka. Standing shoulder-high in the brush, Dave and I loosed a shot or two and brought the hind down. We stripped all the venison from the deer and smashed back to the trail to cache it. Two pighunters from Napier, with their team of dogs, had followed our track, so we yarned before they plunged into the scrub.

The valley was undulating, but the dense manuka had swamped the grass and engulfed the fences. Dave and I pushed through to an ancient pine plantation where the long abandoned Ngatapu homestead still huddled forlornly. Forty, perhaps fifty old deer antlers adorned the sagging fences, and snaggle-toothed boar-heads had been nailed atop each strainer post. I was more interested in the old ram horns, spiralling in spectacular circuits.

There were a lot of utensils, even an expensive double-burner spirit stove still cluttering the dismal shack. That seemed odd until Dave explained that the last occupant had departed hurriedly one jump ahead of a police posse.

Ngatapu homestead had an interesting chequered history. Prior to 1931 the house was sited down on a terrace by the fast-flowing Hautapu Stream. The river winds through a tremendous chasm in the granite range to the east, and during the upheaval of the disastrous Hawke's Bay earthquake of 1931, a whole precipice plunged into the canyon, damming the whole stream. The water backed up for miles, flooding out the homestead. The house was jacked on to logs and floated to the high escarpment it now occupies. Ngatapu sheep station was one of the most remote and inaccessible in the North Island and wool went out by pack train seven or eight miles down to ford the Mohaka, and then by the long trail winding through the scrub to Te Pohue on the Napier-Taupo road.

In 1938 the station was finally abandoned to the encroaching manuka, the wild pigs and deer, and the remaining Merino sheep left to roam wild. There is a deep grass gorge close to the homestead, rimmed with manuka, the last stronghold of the wild rams of Ngatapu. Dave and I tramped through the scrub and crept to peep through the fringe. There were twenty or thirty wild sheep in sight, grazing in small bands or lying in the noonday sun. Most were immature sheep or ewes with young lambs at foot. An odd fact is that the main lambing period appears to have reverted to mid-June. We glassed the sheep thoroughly, noted an old set of bleaching deer antlers across the gorge, and several rams wandering in the distant thickets. Growth of horns didn't appear outstanding.

On an adjacent spur there was a movement in the scrub and an ancient Merino ram, crippled with foot rot, hobbled on to a sunny knoll. His was a trophy set of horns, spiralling in tight curves. We crept down into the gully, carefully sneaked past a mob of ewes and lambs, climbed to a razor-sharp spur. The range wasn't long, perhaps 200 yards, and my rifle spoke but once.

Dave swung round to aim at a hogget, for wild Merino meat is delicious. The wild bands of sheep are constantly attacked by neighbouring farmers, who don't appreciate the attentions the wily rams pay their tame ewe flocks. My ram was infested with ticks too, which are not over-popular with the farming community.

The wild sheep of Shangri-la have escaped much attention up till the present, their hideout has been so remote. But Ngatapu is, I gather, now being developed for farming. Soon the pigs and deer, wild cattle and Merinos of Shangri-la will be gone for ever, destroyed by bulldozer, bullet, and barbed wire.

New Zealand's Toughest Trophy

WHICH IS THE HARDEST TYPE of New Zealand game animal to hang on the wall? Is it a respectable red, a good set of boar tusks or a nimble buck chamois? Or perhaps a sika stag or a whitetail buck?

Now let us consider what constitutes a trophy. It's a bit like collecting blondes—beauty is very much in the eye of the beholder. I have guided several parties of Americans hunting in New Zealand and they really cherish those big grey wallaby from the Hunter Hills and take them proudly home for a costly full-size life mount. But Kiwis don't rate the wallaby a trophy at all.

I have heard it expounded, with considerable sympathy, that a hunting trophy is anything that a stalker treasures as a remembrance of a stalk. After all, a miserable six-point red stag, shot by an excited lad on his first hunt, is probably more of a trophy to him than a sixteen-pointer to a seasoned stalker with a whole room full of other fine heads.

For the sake of this chapter we have to draw the line somewhere, so I'd suggest that a trophy is a mature head of its species —something the average stalker would be proud to display and that might win a prize at New Zealand Deerstalkers' Association branch level.

I'm going to put thar, chamois, wild boar, Angora goat, and seven species of deer on my trophy list. The deer are fallow, red, rusa, samba, sika, wapiti, and whitetail.

It could be argued, and I'll agree, that in some circumstances a wild sheep and wild bull could be trophies. So could a wapiti-red hybrid stag. And what about moose and axis? I have no doubts about erasing the axis (or chital) as I don't believe an authentic specimen has been seen or shot since the original release. Certainly I'm aware that a veteran Bulls stalker, now deceased, believed he had shot a chital stag in 1948 and the mounted head is now in Wanganui Museum. I saw hundreds of axis deer in India, and shot several, and I'm quite certain the Wanganui specimen is no axis. There may still be a bull moose in Fiordland, but I would rather protect than shoot the last lone bull.

Of our eleven trophies I believe a good tusker might be the surest bet. After all, wherever you live there are wild pigs, often easily accessible. Four or five hours' hard driving from anywhere in New Zealand should have you nearing pig country.

I was doubtful whether to include the goat, but there is a national trophy for the best set of horns. There are goats all over New Zealand too. They are easy to spot and stalk, but shooting a takeable trophy, with plenty of curl and a thirty-inch spread, may take lots of mileage and investigation. For instance there are thousands of goats in the Wakatipu area, but I've never seen one billy around there carrying decent horns.

A bull thar with a twelve-inch horn isn't too hard to find. The country they frequent in the Southern Alps is open and you can spot them for miles. Climb high and you'll shoot your bull, maybe several if you wish. I'm aware that thar-hunting involves considerable travel for a North Island stalker, but so does a whitetail and wapiti trip. On the other hand, remember the South Island man has to go north for his sika, samba and rusa. Possibly a big bull thar could be the country's easiest trophy, ahead of boar and goat.

A nine-inch chamois is a more chancy trophy, but they range over much of the South Island and many good chamois trophies are taken by men stalking for red deer. If you spend only a week in good chamois country, stalking them, you could quite possibly shoot four or five nine-inch bucks, and maybe a ten-inch, or better.

I believe that a reasonable red is the easiest of the seven deer, partly because of their wide range. Not too many heads are taken in the North Island now, but I suppose there are twenty trophies shot with twelve points or better and a combined length and spread of seventy inches. Mind you I have measured a West

Taupo red with seventeen great tines, spread thirty-nine and a half inches and length forty-five inches. I'd guess at another 180 shot in the South Island—200 altogether. After all, there could be around 200,000 red deer shot annually, making one trophy in a thousand.

A sika or Japanese stag from south-east of Taupo is a wily trophy, but a considerable number of good sika trophies turn up each year at New Zealand Deerstalkers' Association functions at the Waikato, Putaruru, Hawke's Bay and many other branches. We will give our sika trophy eight points and a length of, say, twenty-six inches.

The last four or five trophies are the tougher ones. These days a good fallow buck is a rare specimen. This is a breed that the venison hunters are eliminating, for our fallow herds are all isolated and have retreated to relatively small areas such as the Blue Mountains, Lower Wanganui River, Mt Creighton, and the Greenstone-Caples herd to the west. Much of the fallow territory is barred to all but a few stalkers and trophies these days are scarce. Few fallow heads with fair palmation, fifteen or sixteen points and spread and length of fifty inches are shot these days.

Now to consider the wapiti. Terrain and climate are some of the most forbidding in New Zealand, but provided you can draw a block and spend three weeks there, you should take a bull with twelve points and length and spread combined of ninety inches. There must be six or eight such heads or better brought out each year.

How many reasonable whitetail are shot each season? Quite frankly I don't know, but I have seen many more wapiti heads than whitetails. I note that Allan Harrison believes 1,200 or more whitetail are shot each year on Stewart Island. This is a large number. I hunted there in April 1966. I found the bush stalking open and pleasant, but access by Stewart Island ferry and fishing craft was uncertain and time-consuming. At least a dozen reasonable whitetail heads, length and spread combined—say thirty-two inches, carrying eight points, are shot each season, for I saw six good trophies in the fish freezer, all shot by Half Moon Bay commercial fishermen. Right now, there are more whitetail than wapiti trophies being taken, but the whitetails are hunted much more intensively.

You should take a wapiti in three weeks, but you will be very fortunate to take a whitetail in the same period. Is that a fair summing up? Note, I haven't mentioned the small Wakatipu whitetail herd, for I haven't hunted there. Stalking the herd is severely restricted, though I believe the heads may be superior to those of Stewart Island.

Now for the two toughest trophies, samba and rusa. Which is the harder to take?

To take a rusa stag in daylight is a real challenge, and several farmers at Galatea with rusa deer on their small dairy properties have hunted intensively for years and still haven't shot one. Recently my mate Russell Sattrup displayed a rusa at the dinner of the Waikato Branch of the Deerstalkers, and it was the first rusa to come forward for Waikato competition in four or five years. They're a rare and valued trophy all right. Size of a rusa head? I've heard a rusa trophy defined as "any stag with horns on", but if you can take one with six points and a length of twenty inches, you'll be hunting hard and long.

I'm a fairly experienced rusa stalker by now, but it took seven trips before I shot my trophy. The rusa habitat is shockingly difficult country—interlaced bracken and manuka ten feet high, on the precipitous Urewera slopes above the cow farms. A dull brown colour all over, the Javan rusa blends perfectly with the scrub. His nerve and skill at lying hidden is remarkable. A contractor was crushing a patch of scrub, smashing round and round the block, and when the dozer was levelling the last long strip in the centre, a fine rusa buck leapt from under the blade.

The samba is the one species I haven't stalked in New Zealand, mainly because I shot a fine 40 x 40 specimen in India. Land development around Rotorua and the Mt Tarawera region is eroding the last samba strongholds of the north. I've handled three good heads taken by Government deer cullers from Te Teko, near Whakatane, and there are still samba in the sandhills of the Manawatu coast. I think most trophies up north are shot by chance when hunting pigs or other game, or else taken by spotlighters.

In the Manawatu some samba are shot by drives, a couple of stalkers rousing the valley in the sandhills while their mates wait with ready rifles.

I believe a samba may be New Zealand's toughest trophy and the following chapter reinforces this view.

On the Trail of a Samba Stag

THE SAMBA is one of New Zealand's largest deer, almost the size of a wapiti, but probably the least-sighted species of all. Samba are thinly scattered, cunning, and nocturnal in their feeding habits. I stalked and shot fine samba stags in India, and so rather neglected the New Zealand herd until quite recently.

Mick Marshall, an Angus stud breeder from Ashcott, remarked that he would arrange a Manawatu hunt for me, and a few weeks later we motored over one evening. The Manawatu herd live on a strip of scrubby sandhills along the coast, in a curving arc from Foxton up to Wanganui. Lupins, gorse, manuka, fern, and marram grass clothe the sandy hummocks, and pines have also been planted extensively.

Samba occasionally horn a few pine trees and are not over-popular with the foresters. But as the plantations are alive with various contractors—felling, thinning, clearing scrub, planting or re-planting—all daylight hunting is absolutely barred, and only very limited spotlight shooting allowed.

Our Manawatu hosts were the forestry foreman, Wally Ingram, and a couple of his friends, Leo and John. It was an extremely dark September evening, and there was a hint of rain in the air as the stubby landrover nosed up to the locked gates. Hanging on the fence were the head and antlers of a small six-point samba stag shot in the plantation the previous week. Up and down the logging roads the spotlight swept the sombre pines. Here and there amber-eyed opossum scuttled for cover, but of deer we saw none. Occasional deer tracks or droppings showed on the trail, and out in the young pines to the west few trees had been barked. An interesting but fruitless experience.

My next venture after samba was further north. There are a few samba in the pine forests of Kaingaroa, northwards from the Napier-Taupo road to the volcanic wastes of Mt Tarawera near Rotorua, and eastwards towards Te Teko and Taneatua in the Bay of Plenty. Arranging likely samba-hunting country in the north was frustrating. The Land and Survey Department's development blocks barred access to their territory and the scrublands beyond, and after fruitless enquiries and correspondence,

Russell Sattrup and I decided to rendezvous at Galatea and see what we could find from there.

I remembered three fine samba heads which Alan Rhea had once displayed to me at the Horomanga Forestry Headquarters. Two were good six-point trophies and the other carried an unusual extra tine to make seven points. All three stags had been shot down the Rangataiki River near Te Teko.

Russell and I pitched camp at our familiar site in the Horomanga. It was too late to go on to the Bay of Plenty on a more or less blind quest that day; better, we decided, to enquire around Te Teko next morning. Russell took his Stiga rifle and climbed across the river while I tackled the high mountain south of the river. It was well-remembered territory which we had both hunted many times for rusa, but neither of us was seriously hunting on this occasion. I spent a while stalking a little group of four cautious rusa does with the camera. They lived in a sheltered hollow near the crest of the mountain, an area rich in tall kanuka trees and luxuriant toe-toe bushes. I've seen the same deer over several years—wary, inquisitive little faces peeping through the toe-toes.

Russell and I were off down-river next morning towards samba territory, but it's not tactful to call on a strange farmer before breakfast. Daylight in October is around 5 am, so we went for a quick stroll just to see if there were many rusa about. Stalking along the edge of the scrubline in the tawny light I spied four dark objects out in the fresh spring grass. "Rush bushes," I thought, knowing a damp patch thereabouts. Keeping close to the fenceline and its screening scrub, I walked rapidly closer and realised that the "rush bushes" were drifting toward the fence.

Up came the heavy binoculars, identifying three rusa does and a small six-point rusa stag.

Further along the boundary was another moving animal, large and dark in the dawn's shadows. "That could be an old man stag," I realised, the trophy hunter instinct suddenly awake.

Many times—perhaps on fifty or sixty occasions—have I stalked the fields of Galatea when seriously after a rusa trophy and only once, years before, had I ever seen a stag beyond the scrub.

Well before real daylight the four closest rusa deer were edging toward cover, slipping under the fence. Impatiently I watched them go, walking quietly closer, eager to be past them and after the big, distant animal. The little deer were wandering aimlessly through an opening of fern and scattered manuka but beyond them, deep in the shadow of a kanuka, I glimpsed a big, dark stag, white-tipped antlers tilted far back as the animal watched my way. I dropped the binoculars and quietly worked a shell into the breech. Without the scope sight an accurate shot would have been impossible. When I fired, deer exploded everywhere, darting into the shadows of the scrub.

My eyes were still on the big stag. He rushed across a small grass opening, leapt a fallen tree and, to my dismay, disappeared into dense cover. I ran across, searched, and found no sign of blood. I did a hasty circuit through the bushes, and then made a wider and more thorough search. After rapidly circling a small, dense patch of fern I crashed through it. Up leapt a six-point rusa from where it had been craftily lying. I could have shot it, but knew this was the small stag I had sighted earlier out on the grass. They're cunning, those rusa. It took real nerve, after the herd had been shot at, to sneak into a tiny patch of fern, twenty feet across, and lie hidden while I circled and searched all around.

It must have been nearly an hour before I found my trophy, quite dead, deep in the fern and five-finger trees. The stag was magnificent, carrying six long tines, heavy-beamed, with the curving back turn in the main antlers peculiar to rusa. Entered in the 1968 National Competition of the New Zealand Deerstalkers' Association, my rusa won the year's top trophy in the rusa class and came third equal for the Orbell Trophy, for the premier head of any deer species for 1968.

With an unexpected trophy like that in the bag, and a whole carcass of prime venison wasting in the hot sun, the samba search was somewhat overshadowed. Russell headed for Rotorua to unearth any samba clues he could find on the Tarawera-Rerewhaitu area, while I turned the rover down through the Kaingaroa pines from Murupara. Quite a criss-cross of private forestry roads bisects the forest and fire hazard permitting, the Forestry Headquarters occasionally allow travellers special permits to short cut from Murupara straight through to the Napier-Taupo highway. It must trim forty miles off the main route, quite a saving.

Way down the forestry road where the paved highway had

degenerated to a slippery, pumice trail, I saw the deer I was searching for. Three grey samba does, big round ears aquiver, wheeled across the fire-break and disappeared. They were the first samba deer I'd ever seen in New Zealand and a promising end to my second samba hunt.

"That's right. I took forty-seven rifles across the lake here one weekend last roar, and of course there were other hunters going across in their own boats," ranger Wally Vaughan told me as he piloted the tourist launch.

"Did they shoot anything?"

"Three!"

There were three samba stalkers aboard, Russell, Wilby and myself, and as the tourist season had closed for the 1968 winter, we had had to hire a special return cruise across Lake Tarawera. East of Lake Tarawera sprawl the volcanic wastes of Tarawera mountain, with crest split asunder in the great eruption of 1886. A tourist track runs across a narrow, scrubby ridge to Lake Rotomahana and here Wally put us ashore, with permission to camp in an empty shed.

Cold, blustery wind swept snow-showers across the lake and we were pleased to use the draughty tin shelter. Odd trees were crashing down, and pitching and holding up the pup tents would have been quite difficult.

It was all unfamiliar stalking country, so we split three ways to explore. Russell searched low along the scrubby bush between mountain and lake, and reported numerous fresh deer sign. Wilby swung up a wash to the west, a waste of eroded pumice, crisscrossed with narrow gulches and steep little ravines. Shortly after leaving camp, still quite early in the afternoon, Wilby had an amusing experience. He came to a small, twisting gulch, rich in tutu scrub. It was just too wide to leap comfortably, maybe eight or nine feet across, and about as deep. He slithered down into the cleft and followed the watercourse for a chain or two, looking for a break in the vertical, crumbling walls. A fresh-looking deer's footprint in the damp sand caught his eye.

"That looks mighty new," Wilby thought. "Better get out of this hole and see around."

He clawed up a tutu bush and, maybe twenty yards further along the gulch, a startled five-point red stag was also scrambling out the same side. This was no trophy samba, so Wilby watched

Above: Lloyd Tillett with a sika stag. Note the lightly spotted hide.

The lovely beeches of State Forest 90, south-east of Taupo. This area is a stronghold of the Japanese sika deer.

Above: Two safari groups cross trails. These Americans all came from Pennsylvania, and they met quite by chance on the road near Wairakei. The land-rover belongs to Rex Forrester.

An outstanding rusa trophy shot by the author when he had left home on a samba hunt.

the small stag scamper into the manuka.

I climbed to the sprawling low divide between Lake Tarawera and Lake Rotomahana to the south. Dense manuka and regrowth scrub crowded the ridge, though there were still a few likely grass plots. Wattle was spreading wild across Tarawera, growing quickly and crowding out the native flora.

It was a wild winter night and we planned an early start in the morning. Russell boiled three pounds of saveloys, ready for next day's lunch. The candles wouldn't burn because of the healthy draught and there was one of those not unusual little incidents which happen in the dark. The saveloys went upside down in the cinders, pumice and dirt. We rinsed them in the lake and went to bed.

Russell was up around 5 am swearing violently. A hungry opossum, or maybe a whole tribe of them, had crawled under the iron and eaten all but a saveloy and a half. By daylight the three of us were high on the trail winding up Mt Tarawera. Russell swung aside to stalk down a wide, scrubby valley back to the lake. Wilby decided to search the bush slopes north-east of the same valley, so I climbed high up on to the lava slopes of Tarawera.

West of Mt Tarawera a broad plateau rises steeply two or three hundred feet from the lake, then shelves back gently for a couple of miles before the volcanic cone rears sharply into the sky. Scrub growth and young bush was regenerating vigorously now after the old eruption of 1886, but wandering north below the main cone I was more or less above the timberline. Deer sign was almost non-existent except for a rare odd dropping, usually months old.

The ancient lava flow and subsequent ash fall have eroded rapidly, and winding steep-sided gulches twist haphazardly down to the lake. Later scrub growth has stabilised the stricken area and the whole mountain is a maze of hidden, scrub-covered gulches and canyons.

Tired of climbing into and out of an endless succession of gulches, I angled down towards the lake, becoming tangled in an even worse maze of canyons. Nearer the lake, instead of gulches, there were vertical canyons a hundred, two hundred feet deep. But the bush was higher, more open near the lake, and deer sign was abundant, though the only deer I saw were two or three startled reds. Towards 2 pm I had struggled back near Russell's valley and he frightened three more deer up from below. We all saw deer that day and both Russell and Wilby could have shot several. But none were samba.

The third day was our last, with Wally due at 2 pm with the tourist launch. I searched the dividing ridge again at daybreak, and glimpsed one deer darting through the scrub. Wilby stalked the wash, and decided to try for meat when he saw a young stag in the scrub edge. Wilby described the shot as an easy one, but the red stag disappeared and we could find no sign of blood.

I joined Wilby on a trail through the heavy scrub and we explored an area west of Lake Rotomahana. Shooting near the shore of Rotomahana is banned, so we watched the famed steaming white cliffs for a while, then turned up into a pumice gorge. Blackberry, gorse, fern and manuka clothed the pumice ridges and writhing, narrow canyons. There might have been samba there—we saw none—but we did spot another four or five red deer. There were wild pigs around the Tarawera too and I had even sighted occasional rooting high up the volcano. What the pigs found up in that sterile scoria is hard to imagine, but I'll bet they're a lean brand of porker.

Some time later Mick Marshall and I made another spotlight hunt in the Manawatu with the same hospitable party. We saw no deer but got a bit closer. Dipping into a lupin hollow among the pines, a heavy animal, unseen, crashed through the thickets.

Wally Ingram played the spotlight from a low sandhill, across a tangled swamp rich in toe-toes, cabbage trees, manuka, and lupin.

"Samba in there," he remarked. "Chap saw five one day last week and shot one. We drove a valley further over too and put a couple of rifles on the ridge up front, while Leo and I pushed through. One of the boys up ahead saw a samba hind sneaking past. He waited until he could spot both Leo and me, and shot the doe when we were out of line."

"How would it be if I sat up in a cabbage tree or a sandhill all day in there?"

"That's not our country," replied Wally. "But if I ask I just might get you in."

The chances of shooting a trophy samba by spotlight are remote indeed. Wally and his party see a deer about every third night trip, and shoot a deer—any deer—perhaps one hunt in four. A daylight samba hunt, with a chance to evaluate the trophy before I shot, was more in my line. Spotlight hunting is fine for opossums.

One hot November afternoon the landrover headed for Marton again. Companion on this trip was Allan Duncum, national vice-president of the Deerstalkers' Association. Wally directed us to a small clearing in the pines, where we pitched a spacious tent. Three hours before dark, Allan and I climbed the fence into the adjoining scrub and lupin dunes and settled to wait, each on a commanding hummock. It was a pleasant vigil, watching the proud pheasant and droll hares. But of samba we saw none.

The Americans greatly favour this method of waiting, hidden on a stand—"still-hunting" it is called in the States. But Allan and I had had enough of sitting about. Next morning we were away at first light, prowling the scrubby wastes. On a low, sandy ridge I noted the bleaching antlers of a big samba stag, shot years before in velvet. Occasionally I noted droppings or hoof marks of samba, and once a samba deer crashed away. It must have watched me from close by in dense manuka, but the only thing I saw was waving brush.

An hour after sunrise I heard the sharp report of Allan's .270. He had sighted a samba all right and shot it too, a prime young doe. We gave a heavy haunch to Wally Ingram and headed the rover toward Hawke's Bay.

So I'm still on the trail of a samba stag, and somewhere, some place, some time, I'll meet up with one!

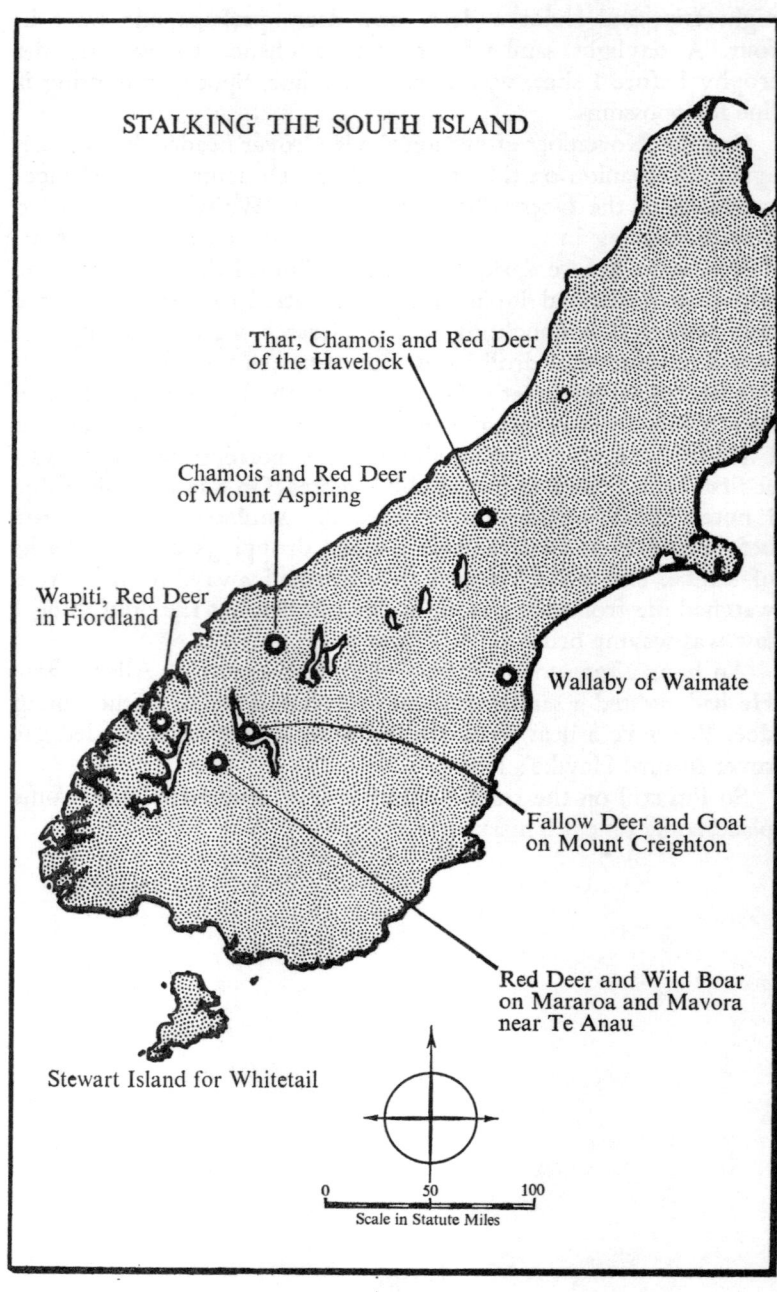

PART III
SOUTHLAND AND STEWART ISLAND

The Mountains of Mavora

YARNING COMFORTABLY, with a mug of whisky or rum apiece, five of us sat around the fire in crude Bushcreek Hut, far up the Mararoa Valley. There was Paul Ilgenfritz from America, Allan Bradley and John MacDonald from the Te Anau area, and Denis Oliver and I from Hawke's Bay.

Allan Bradley, owner of Mararoa Station, had kindled my interest in the remote Whitestone River when he remarked that it would be an interesting traverse from the vicinity of the Mavora Lakes, over the lonely Livingstone Mountains to the west, then down the forested Whitestone Valley to the hinterland of Mararoa sheep station.

"There have been a few good heads seen around the head of the West Burn," Allan added.

A year later, Denis and I were headed into the mountains of Mavora. We arrived at the shearers' quarters at Mararoa Station some time about 2 am.

The alarm clock dragged us out at 4.30 am. While Denis fried generous helpings of bacon and eggs, I hurriedly sorted out the supplies and gear needed for a seven- or eight-day tramp into unknown country.

Allan Bradley had arranged to collect us at 7 am but at 5.30 he was stamping in, impatient to be on the long drive north. Hurriedly I tossed some dehydrated potatoes and onion on the pile, a loaf or two of bread, a pound of butter, some fat, and plenty of salt and rice. A carton of eggs came to light. Never before had I carried eggs into the bush, but the idea of fried venison steak and eggs appealed, so without much thought I jammed them atop my pack. A few eggs survived—not many.

By daylight we were on the forty-mile drive up the Mararoa Valley, winding through Burwood Station on the route to Mavora Lakes.

Where the birch forest flows down from the mountains and floods the Mararoa Valley, nestle two lovely stretches of still water, the hidden Mavora Lakes. South Mavora Lake is some four or five miles long and a mile wide, almost surrounded by beautiful birches. Fish abound—giant trout swimming lazily in the clear mountain water.

North Mavora Lake is somewhat larger, perhaps ten miles long. A mile or so of river joins the two lakes and, across the deep, swift Mararoa the deerstalkers have constructed a narrow swing-bridge. Here Allan deposited us, then drove on to leave mail and supplies for the boundary rider on Burwood Station. Burwood is probably the only station in New Zealand to warrant a boundary rider; all summer a Burwood shepherd rides herd on thousands of ewes on unfenced open ranges. The ewes, surprisingly enough, are all Romneys.

With a rendezvous arranged across the range in the Whitestone Valley eight days later, Allan Bradley bumped away in my landrover. Denis Oliver and I swayed over the timber bridge, then plunged into the Southland birch forest. Gradually the slope steepened until we were scrambling up through the birches, swinging from tree to tree, clawing at the roots. In an hour and a half, in spite of the heavy packs on our backs, we had pushed through the last trees and climbed across a bluff on to a snowgrass ledge.

The view was glorious. Ahead stretched the mountains of Mavora, tussock ridges spilling down from the range ahead. Below lay the twin jewel lakes of Mavora, bright blue, surrounded by sombre bush or bright yellow tussock.

We climbed steadily and from a near frozen tarn ringed with banks of crisp snow we sipped a mug of icy water, and chewed a slice or two of bread in the lee of a huge rock. Near the crest of the range snow lay deep in wind-driven drifts. Thankfully we cast the weighty packs aside and groped for our cameras. I saw Denis crouch, dash for his rifle. I ran to meet him, scooping up my BSA 30.06 and binoculars.

"A big stag lying in the hollow," Denis grunted. "Hasn't seen me. Three points on each top."

"Okay," I said. "He's yours. But I want a photo first before you shoot."

In the snowgrass basin below, sheltered from the gale, were two stags. One, grazing, was a smallish nine-pointer, while the big stag lay drowsing, sixty or seventy yards below. I took my photos, then Denis's .303 cracked once. We watched the other beast go, then ran down to the trophy. Although heavily timbered, one bay tine was missing, to make an eleven points. Several of the tops had been splintered, probably in a fall, and twice bullets had recently drilled through the main beam. Denis tied the antlers on his pack, then we slogged into the wind on to the exposed western shoulder of the range, above the headwaters of the Whitestone Valley.

Allan had given us some rather vague instructions about an ancient, long disused, mustering bivvy somewhere in the bush edge of the Upper Whitestone, so we prowled back and forth through four or five acres of birches which fitted his directions. Finally, as a rain squall swirled down from the peaks, we pitched the tent. Boulders strewed the ground and even a piece of ground four feet by six feet was far from level. By torch and firelight we strung up a shelter, fried a pan full of steak, then propped a log on the lower side of our tent to stop us from rolling out in the night.

Before dawn we cooked another pan of venison steak each and were on the hunting trail before sunrise. Denis decided to stalk an isolated mountain across the Whitestone known as East Burwood, while I headed up the Whitestone Valley, north toward the West Burn Saddle.

The Upper Whitestone is on the southern edge of a vast area of sprawling snowgrass mountains extending toward Lake Wakatipu, twenty miles to the north. Under the West Burn Saddle there is a bench, angling at a handy angle up toward the saddle itself. I was halfway up the climb when I spied a stag directly above, 1,000 feet higher, hiding among a scattering of boulders on the brink of a cliff. The glasses showed only a six-point head so I watched him for a while, rather amused, for the beast was obviously hiding from me, not realising that I could see him. I crept to the edge of my bench, scanned the valley curving into the mountain peaks, and saw another stag with a more promising head grazing near the stream a mile up the valley. Stalking closer

I walked unseen up the ledge until I reached a promontory some 400 yards from the animal.

I edged over the rocks, expecting the stag to be still grazing peacefully below, but he was in full flight, galloping across the shingle, leaping the stream in a wild bound. With the big binoculars I watched him run, then gradually slow to a walk and climb to a little herd of deer. Three of the five deer he met soon became uneasy at his dying panic, and joined him to climb slowly toward the skyline ridge. But the two remaining beasts, one a heavy limping stag, walked up through the rocks, then settled to browse. The two stags were far away, barely discernible to the unaided eye, but the limping stag appeared to carry an interesting set of antlers.

Through the 20 X binoculars I strained to count the tines, and decided there were four points on one top, three on the other. After him I went, plunging down across the valley, sweating up through the snowgrass, straining to cross and climb high above before another wandering gust of air caught my scent and warned them, as it had warned the other stag before.

Rifle loaded, I crept through the snowgrass, peeping over the last low brow. The limping stag *did* have three and four points on each royal and was just dropping over a ridge some 150 yards distant.

Bang. Missed.

Bang again. Realising I had shot too hurriedly, that the magazine was nearly empty and the last bullet had to count, I steadied, then brought the animal down. It was an interesting set of antlers, but no trophy. Certainly the white-tipped royals, three and four to a side, were there curving backwards but the lower tines were either lacking entirely or woefully stunted. He was an old stag, and had limped for many years, for one front leg was missing below the knee. It had completely healed long ago, and had grown a thick pad of sinew.

Denis turned up quite unexpectedly and together we climbed high into the headwaters of the Whitestone, and in the teeth of a screaming gale we fought our way over the crest of 5,491-foot high Mt Richmond, the highest peak in the vicinity. During the day we sighted the missing bivvy in the birch fringes on a bench high above the river so, late in the evening, we gathered our tent and gear and climbed to the crude shelter.

Long ago when Burwood Station summer-grazed the Whitestone headwaters, a few rolled sheets of flat iron had been packed in on horseback. The bivvy was some six feet by eight, barely high enough to squat upright in, with a tiny fireplace and small hole alongside which served as both door and window. We cut fresh snowgrass for bedding, and crammed a heap of firewood in one corner.

Snow and rain slashed our camp all night but eased toward dawn. Denis and I then hunted southwards up a winding snowgrass valley which climbed into the peaks of Mavora. It was some hours before any interesting game was sighted, three stags high on the ridge above. They were too distant to count the points, though two carried a fine spread. Keeping in the shelter of a snowgrass crevice we climbed rapidly and trod softly on to a commanding rocky knob. The deer were quite close, two excellent young eight-pointers and, lower down, a ten-pointer with long curving tines. I took several photographs, then as the stags started to trot away, Denis whispered:

"Shoot the big ten, Keith. I already have my eleven to carry out."

I shot—missed.

"Over the top," gasped Denis.

The stag went down next bullet, but the target had been an easy one and I was somewhat disgruntled at missing again. The 30.06 had been shooting extremely well when I had been guiding earlier with Bill Koller, often at very long range, but now I was putting my close shots over the deer.

On the high exposed ridge above the Whitestone the wind was overwhelming. Reeling in the howling gale, Denis and I fought our way across the summit of Mt Cerebus. We were finally flung over the crest into the sheltered lee of a craggy, jagged rock pile. We crouched there awhile, then, the day almost gone, we tramped toward camp.

The wind died away during the hours of night and by dawn glistening hoar frost dusted the snowgrass. Denis crossed the Whitestone Stream to climb on to East Burwood Mountain again and hunt north, while I climbed the mountain directly behind our bivvy along the jagged crest of the range.

Mt Eldon, a scarred rocky peak, reared ahead. I tried to skirt its western flanks by sidling high above the Whitestone Gorge, but deep ragged rock chutes—sheer and impassable—forced me to climb higher, zigzagging upwards to the peak through the rocks and soft snow. Mt Eldon, 5,470 feet high, is a spectacular pinnacle peak, so sharp on the highest tip there was barely room to lay aside the little stalking rucksack and my firearm.

I felt a little like Ed Hillary atop Everest, nothing but fresh air all around and no visible means of support. The view was absolutely glorious but after a few photos and a biscuit on my eyrie I rather cautiously and precariously climbed down through the crags, where a false step right or left would send me hurtling 1,000 feet.

I had been tramping for four or five hours before I sighted game, a little herd of three or four deer drowsing in the golden snowgrass toward North Mavora Lake. A mile further north there were another two young stags grazing in a steep basin. I watched them for a while from my perch on the rim rock, then wandered on along the crest, with the long narrow North Mavora Lake on my right and the headwaters of the West Burn Stream to the left.

A high snowgrass knob falling almost sheer some 3,500 feet into Mavora barred my way, so instead of climbing the mountain, I scrambled around it to the west.

I was stepping across a loose shingle slide when I froze, and sank slowly to the gravel, grasping for the binoculars swinging loose around my neck. There was a stag—a beauty—lying asleep on a rocky prominence far below. With his head and heavy antlers stretched out, resting sprawled on the ground, I thought for a long moment the stag was dead. Then he twitched an ear and lifted his majestic head to search the valley beneath. I totalled fourteen points, seven long, sharp, curving tines on each antler to make the rare Imperial.

I crouched motionless until the stag relaxed again, then slid slowly to the nearest boulder and steadied my wrist atop it. The range didn't appear too distant, about 250 yards I estimated, down and across the slide. The stag's body appeared to be partly hidden by the sparse snowgrass and as I had shot too high on the only two Mavora stags I had shot previously, I determined not to make the same mistake again. Aiming just where the stag's shoulder seemed to disappear in the vegetation, I squeezed the trigger.

THE MOUNTAINS OF MAVORA

As the gunshot roared out I was appalled to see the great deer leap to his feet and, in one lithe movement, spring madly down and away, hurtling through the snowgrass in gigantic bounds. Almost before the stag had disappeared I was bounding desperately after him across the rock slide. For five long minutes my rifle barrel swung its dark muzzle up and down the mountain, then I straightened and jerked the bolt open to remove the live 30.06 shell from the firing chamber. The brass cartridge case flung wide, leaving a smear of powder grains in the breech.

Powder, live powder! I snatched up the unfired shell which, sure enough, was minus the bullet. The bullet was wedged firmly in the breech. Savagely I rammed the defective cartridge case back into the firing chamber. But the cartridge case only crumpled and the bolt wouldn't turn down by a quarter inch. I was appalled, for the rifle was completely useless.

Rummaging through my tiny emergency kit containing waterproof matches and a few essential odds and ends, plus an aperture sight for the 30.06, I remembered a little pair of pliers required to fit the spare rear sight. I grabbed them and twisted and wrenched at the brass neck of the shell to tear the moulded case back. The mutilated cartridge slid reluctantly into the chamber and the bolt swung shut.

I glanced once more around the mountain. Still no stag in sight. Much of the powder had been lost, and accuracy and range would be questionable, so I determined to test fire and clear the chamber. I placed the rifle on the ground, planted a hefty boulder atop it, tied a six foot piece of string to the trigger and pulled.

Click! There was no explosion, only the anti-climax of a defective primer. I attacked a new cartridge, loosened and removed the bullet and again tore the brass neck away. As I jerked the trigger the 30.06 jumped with recoil, but the barrel was clear. I scooped up the rifle, glanced around to see if the echoing shot had flushed my stag from hiding and lifted the bolt to replenish the magazine.

The bolt came away in my hand! Something had sheared off inside the mechanism, and if I fired there was no spring or protecting flange to prevent the firing pressure on the bolt-head throwing it back in my eye. With a strong piece of twine I tied the bolt down firmly to the trigger guard.

I hoped the trophy stag was still close by in the valley below. From my ridge I could watch the open range for miles, and I certainly hadn't seen the stag escape, though there was a considerable basin below my bluff which I hadn't yet searched.

My stag was gone. Carefully, cautiously, I reconnoitred the valley and finally descended to the rock where the stag had lain. My bullet mark showed where it had gouged the hard earth, but instead of the stag's body being partly hidden by snowgrass there was practically no screening cover. It certainly appeared as if I had aimed and hit, just too low. I had underestimated the range too, for distance was around 350 yards, perhaps further.

I searched for betraying blood spots, found none, so followed the stag's panic-stricken hoof marks fruitlessly down the West Burn. Sadly I climbed the valley again to stalk the crest of the range until abruptly the West Burn turns east and cuts through to Lake Mavora.

There are two sequels to this day's hunting and, in fairness, I should break the narrative and mention them here.

First about the rifle. When the trip was over I sent the 30.06 away and BSA not only supplied and fitted a new bolt, but also a complete new barrel and action, gratis. That was more than fair.

The fourteen-pointer head may yet be recovered too. A few months later Southland stalker Allan Harrison remarked to me:

"Keith, I hear when the Burwood shepherds were doing their autumn muster up the West Burn they found your fourteen-pointer lying dead."

Wind shook and rattled our bivvy on the fifth morning of our hunt, but the venison steak had been fried and eaten before dawn and by daylight my mate and I had our gear packed and were hiking down the Whitestone. We skidded steeply into the gorge, and turned abruptly into the sombre birches to seek a track down-river. Presently the valley opened into a delightful tussock clearing which wound for miles along the river between thousands of acres of forest.

We chose a lovely spot to camp near the forks of the Whitestone, on a birch terrace just above the stream. With the camp snug, we waded the Whitestone, plunged into the forest and climbed on to Mt Snowdon. Snowdon is a peculiar mountain; a giant whaleback ridge heaving out of the surrounding forest, a lonely mountain apart from the main range, capped with a few thousand acres of snowgrass and rock above the bushline.

Crouching in whatever sheltered ledges and hollows we could find, Denis and I doggedly slogged toward the peak, fighting a hurricane, but determined to reach the summit and see what lay beyond. On a high shoulder of our spur the wind was shrieking over, whipping an endless hail of small stones and dust ahead of it. During countless years the wind had gouged out an arid gully in the bedrock, some twenty feet deep and a hundred feet wide. The windlashed debris had spilled down into the tossing snowgrass. Never had I seen a wind slash like that before.

The gale tunnelling through that hollow must have exceeded 100 miles per hour. We literally couldn't crawl into it, so detoured way below the scattered debris to avoid the blast. By a tarn 1,000 feet below the summit I saw an odd shining object in the snowgrass, investigated, and found the weathered antlers of an old twelve-point stag.

A spiker had been huddling miserably by a heavy boulder but he didn't like our distant approach and climbed into the upper basin, disturbing several stags sheltering there. Glassing with the gale was difficult but they appeared to be wide-antlered eight-pointers, with the possible exception of one which might have carried ten points. The ten-pointer butted at another stag and lifted his head to roar, but with the wind we sensed rather than heard him. Though 23 March, it was the only roar we heard on the entire trek.

The deer went over the skyline and we tried to follow, then abandoned the chase and swung north just under the crest. Hunting was hopeless, so we scrambled thankfully into the next basin, descending swiftly towards the forest far below.

The South Island beech bush is fairly free of undergrowth so we made fast time and pushed into the snowgrass flats of the Whitestone in the dusk. There were two or three deer grazing near the river, so Denis aimed at a yearling and shot it for camp meat. Paradise duck flew down the Whitestone ahead of us and half a dozen friendly bush robins flitted about the campfire and hopped dangerously close to the burning embers.

After a wet and stormy night the dawn was clear so we parted, Denis climbing through a broad belt of forest back on to the Mavora tussock tops. I crossed the Whitestone River and climbed high through the birches to explore the southern slopes of Mt

Snowdon. The wind increased alarmingly, and on the skyline the gale was the worst I'd ever experienced. I couldn't stand up, I couldn't crawl, and finally I tried to wriggle across the crest into the teeth of the hurricane on my stomach, clutching the stunted vegetation to hold myself to the ground.

During a slight lull (the wind perhaps eased from 120 to 100 miles per hour) I crawled over and scuttled hastily among some boulders. Later when we reached civilisation I learnt that on that particular day New Zealand had experienced tremendous gales everywhere, and that Eyre Forest in North Canterbury had been uprooted.

The beech forest was dangerous, the ground carpeted with fallen twigs. Great branches were being constantly torn off the trees so I didn't linger there.

At daybreak next morning we broke camp, slipped into the straps on our packs and tramped down the river. Denis and I paused once to glance at a very old fourteen-point set of antlers, and later I noted two stags browsing, a spiker and a six-pointer. I wriggled the camera from my pack (it was raining a little) and crept stealthily through the trees toward them. Thirty yards away I took a picture. Still they grazed undisturbed so I crawled to the last birch, fifteen yards distant. The Whitestone Stream burbled between and I had reached as far as I could. Click of camera. The six-pointer threw up his antlers and leapt into the trees.

The valley broadened and we tramped into a large tussock clearing which sprawls across the Whitestone Valley. Though it was now a hot noonday, a sedate hind and fawn grazed quietly in the tussock. I crept close and photographed them before we began looking for a Mararoa outstation shack known as "Igly". Hidden atop a steep little knoll among the birches, it wasn't easy to find. Gratefully we lowered the packs from aching shoulders and reached for the billy.

Igly was a crude and interesting structure, with low walls of rounded beech saplings cut from the surrounding forest, the larger crevices roughly jammed with rotting newspapers. The roof and chimney were of galvanised flat iron, which had been transported in, rolled up, by pack train. There was no floor of course, or door either, except a hanging grain sack flapping forlornly in the breeze. But a warm possie on a wild night and personally I'd rather squat by a log fire in Igly after a day's stalking and swap hunting stories, than lounge in the luxurious beach palaces of Hawaii.

Toward dusk Denis crossed the Whitestone flats while I climbed a tussock hill on the bush edge. Spying north across the Whitestone I could see a large herd of Hereford cattle and a few deer grazing close to the shelter of the birches, but of stags I saw no sign. A movement six or seven miles downstream, yes, that was a landrover, jolting and swaying up the tussock trail, criss-crossing the river. Allan Bradley was on his way.

I surprised a movement on the sprawling flats at the base of the hill and spied two large pigs fossicking. A really big wild boar would find a niche on my trophy room wall, so down I hurried before Allan's jeep disturbed them.

The two pigs were grubbing in the rushes, mangling the carcass of a long-dead sheep. Neither were trophies, being a pair of ugly wild sows, with long, tapering Captain Cooker snouts. I had seldom photographed a wild pig, except bailed, so I sneaked close with the camera poised and took two successful exposures from only sixty feet away. I watched them trot off, then angled across to intercept Allan.

Hanging up our rifles we settled in to empty a bottle of rum and shoot every stag in Southland all over again. We crawled into the sleeping bags eventually, but well before daylight the three of us were awake, wandering about, brewing a billy of tea and making toast.

"If we headed downstream now, we would hit the Prospect Flats just about dawn," remarked Allan. "Just between you and me, there has been a good stag grazing the swedes there lately. Saw him a couple of times in the velvet and let him go."

The sky was inky black with a damp breeze as we weaved the rover downstream. Rain lashed the vehicle as we swung through the gate by the swedes and drove the truck on to a rise to search the crop. There were no deer there that cold, wet dawn so we reversed and skidded our way along the fenceline.

The rover dipped into a shallow depression and almost rammed a huge wild boar rooting the soft damp earth. The pig dived for the fenceline and the manuka beyond, but Allan slipped the jeep between, yelling exultantly. The boar darted towards the back of the rover and before I could leap out with the rifle Allan had reversed violently, heading the furious boar again. Grunting ferociously the big black pig wheeled and hurtled through the fence.

That was the last game we saw. Stalking was over until the following season.

The One That Got Away!

THERE WAS NEVER A STAG in the bush as big as the one that got away! Sixteen-pointers, eighteens—none that I've heard of yet carried only a meagre twelve points. We've all seen or hunted that monster stag and lost him for ever, and the glimpse of a tremendous rack of antlers on the skyline, or crashing through the bush is an elusive memory—a dream we'll never forget.

There is a magnificent red stag still reigning way up a branch of the Mararoa River in Southland. I carried a rifle too, had my chance to shoot; but instead, after a long, long look turned away and went back for my companion.

That phase of the trip had started the previous day, when late in the afternoon I swung my rover past the red-painted woolshed of Mararoa sheep station to greet Allan Bradley. Our party were completing a 2,000-mile safari, starting at Auckland five weeks previously, hunting right down through the North and South Islands. My client at the time was Paul Ilgenfritz. Denis Oliver, my mate from Hawke's Bay, was with us once more. Allan Bradley had expected us over from Queenstown the previous day and had his own short wheel-based landrover loaded and impatient to roll. Allan's tall mate, John McDonald, joined us. Sheep dogs leapt in, licking everyone's face quite impartially while the two rovers convoyed up the broad Mararoa Valley, forded the river to Burwood and bumped forty miles north past the remote and lovely Mavora Lakes. Twin jewels of clear blue mountain water, set amid birches and towering peaks, the Mavora Lakes are, as I've already said, incredibly beautiful.

THE ONE THAT GOT AWAY!

A few miles beyond North Mavora where the Swinton Stream forks aside is a large chunk of birch bush—an isolated lonely forest of a few hundred acres known as Deserters' Bush. During World War I a party of army deserters hid out there. Now the last few fallow deer, remnants of the previous vast Mararoa herds, shelter in Deserters' Bush. We saw several of the little dark deer there a few days later.

A trail of sorts zigzags up the Swinton, weaving between the swampy hollows and tall snowgrass. Twice when Allan's rover shuddered and halted, its chassis caught on huge boulders, it had to be jacked up and the stone pried loose. We dipped to cross the turbulent Swinton at a horrible, deep, boulder-strewn ford. Allan grounded again in midstream, and we waded in, lifted, heaved, and shoved him clear. My longer wheeled-based rover seemed to have more clearance, for I shuddered over.

The night was spent at the Forks Hut, a rough, dark, musterers' shanty. There was a huge fireplace (but no trees within miles so we had carted firewood along with us), half a dozen sagging sack bunks, and a tiny and quite inadequate window. Three or four very old and mouldy sheepskins added a distinctive aroma. Construction was the usual unlined corrugated iron on a frame of trimmed birch saplings. I suppose the Forks shack has seen seventy or eighty winters and will stand a long while yet, haven for the stalker and occasional shepherd.

We were all on the hunting trail before daylight. The weather was perfect, stars shining from a cloudless sky. John McDonald and Allan decided to stalk to the headwaters of a wide canyon which joins the Swinton from the north.

The remaining three of us, Paul, Denis and I, explored the main stream, hunting north-west toward the Upukerora Divide. The treeless valley is a couple of miles broad, flanked by sheer mountains, so Denis stayed near the Swinton while Paul and I stalked along under the base of the cliffs, a mile higher on the mountain slope. My American client was keen enough, but he found the going really tough, particularly on the ragged rock slides spilling out below the cliffs. Denis, way below, rolled a smoke, dawdled, obviously killing time, for he could hardly push ahead and shoot up the valley when it was the American's hunt. Paul and I didn't know it then but Denis could see a huge stag holding five hinds climbing unseen ahead of us. Finally Denis swung aside and disappeared to investigate another snowgrass valley draining far to the south-west.

Paul and I were seeing other game, in fact I was having trouble stopping him from shooting at every stag we saw. Paul already had an eight-point red stag, an unexpected bonus while chamois and thar hunting in the Godley, and now I wanted him to bag a really decent trophy to ship home to the States. About fifteen red deer, hinds, yearlings, and spikers, were moving uneasily ahead of us under the cliffs. There were two six-pointers, one stag with a peculiarly deformed head, carrying one normal antler, the other bending out and down like a bicycle handlebar.

When the deer paused on a sunny tussock spur I managed to get a photo or two, then handled Paul's movie for him to record eight deer filing down the ridge. Photography is part of the job when guiding Americans, apart from skinning and carrying all trophies. Finally the deer circled far enough downwind to catch our scent, and galloped away.

Towards noon Paul and I paused on a steep tussock face. Paul was tiring and I was wondering how much further we could go, pondering the distance back to camp and whether there would be a good stag if I dragged him on to the next spur. Nearby a noisy torrent tumbled down the mountain. There seemed a fair chance that it drained a high basin or hanging valley on the crest of the range so I suggested to Paul that he rest while I investigated. If I saw a trophy worth taking I would signal him up from a bluff 600 feet above.

It took me ten minutes to scale the bluff. There was a glorious basin, a mile deep, luxuriant with snowgrass, rising to a ring of jagged precipices. Much of the basin was obscured by ancient moraine humps so I climbed to a commanding knob, glassed the area thoroughly, then cupped my hands and roared. The cliffs threw back the echo, and I saw a great stag climb unhurriedly to his feet, and stand gazing down toward me. He was absolutely magnificent, carried an enormous set of antlers, curving wide, then up to a cluster of tops.

I focussed the binoculars and gasped at the three great long lower tines, brow, bay and trey, sweeping out and up on each antler. As we were considerably lower than the stag, they showed clearly but the tops were harder to define. All I know is that there was a great mass of curving points on each crown. I have never seen a stag before or since to match that trophy.

The stag wasn't worried—he was something over 400 yards away on a little rocky outcrop under the bluffs. Five hinds grazed nearby, appearing briefly, then wandering out of sight again.

For half an hour I studied that stag, the dream trophy of a lifetime. I carried a scoped 30.06 and could probably have shot the stag from where I was without any great difficulty. There was also the chance, worth investigating, of stalking much closer, up a winding snowgrass depression.

But the stalk or shot wasn't mine to take. The American was paying for the trip, I was the guide and his the chance. Sadly I wriggled back through the screening snowgrass, and descended to wave Paul up. This took some time, but the stag hadn't moved; in fact he had lain down again.

I waited until Paul recovered some breath, checked his Remington, gave a few instructions on keeping under cover, and carefully refrained from mentioning just how large the stag was. I didn't want Paul with a case of buck fever for this was the stag of all stags—monarch of the mountain.

"Paul," I cautioned, "the sun is shining directly our way. You are wearing glasses and I'm wondering if the stag caught a flash of light off my binoculars earlier. He keeps staring this way. Keep well down in the snowgrass, and try and locate him."

Paul reached for the binoculars. "Where? Can't see him . . . which way?"

But the stag was looking too, and never hesitated.

The monarch leapt to his feet, dived over the little knob, hinds gathering as he fled. I had believed I had the whole basin under long-range rifle fire, but there was a shallow unseen depression swinging up toward the skyline. Briefly and occasionally the stag's great antlers showed above the stones as he climbed.

There still appeared nowhere that the stag could climb out through the rim-rock half a mile and more above. That stag wasn't getting away if I could help it.

"Paul," I cried, "I'm going to shoot that stag for you yet if you'll let me."

"Go, Keith, go! I can't climb those peaks ahead. I'm done."

I climbed hard and fast, but somehow, somewhere, that stag escaped. The deer weren't in the next great basin, or the one beyond.

The Case of the Crooked Rifle

I CUPPED MY HANDS and sent an angry bellow echoing across the mountain. But no stag answered my challenge. Far below, sheer down a precipitous bush slope, the East Branch of the Matukituki wound through the birches. Some instinct—the feeling I was being watched—made me swing slowly about. I looked hard into the heavy shadows under the steep rock bluff. I saw a rock there that somehow wasn't a rock, hadn't been there a little earlier when I paused to glass the slope.

A big buck chamois was eyeing me alertly, standing quite still, blending almost perfectly with the cliff. I reached for the 30.06, eased a shell into the breech and, barely moving, raised the heavy weapon to my shoulder. When the gunshot roared out chips of rock flew above the chamois' shoulder. The startled animal leapt six feet toward me, but again my bullet went too high. The buck whirled and fled, springing with incredible ease from rock to crevice. Completely unsettled by missing two easy shots I touched off a third bullet too hurriedly and realised I was missing even as I fired. Now there was only one cartridge left in the rifle.

Chamois have a careless habit of pausing on a prominent rock for one farewell glance backwards and, even as the buck bounded toward the distant crag, my rifle was on him. He paused and, with the sight centred way under the body, I fired my last shot. The animal crumpled and rolled into the snowgrass.

Disgruntled and unhappy with my shooting, I scrambled to the trophy. I have never handled a bigger-bodied chamois. He must have weighed as much as a red hind, though the horns only measured a reasonable nine and a half inches.

With a photo or two recorded I placed the trophy in my little stalking pack and climbed on up into the snowgrass. The weather was deteriorating quickly; cold scuds of rain and snow swirling down from Mt Aspiring just across the valley.

The trip had started a couple of days previously when I had picked up my two mates, Russell Sattrup and Doug Johnston, in Palmerston North. I had been half an hour late for the rendezvous there, but had had to buy a new landrover that morning to head south in, as the gearbox had suddenly packed up in my old one. The stags don't stop roaring while the cogs come out!

THE CASE OF THE CROOKED RIFLE

Down to Wellington, across on the familiar ferry, and by next afternoon we were baptising the new machine in the surging waters of the Matukituki beyond Lake Wanaka.

Mr and Mrs Aspinall of Mt Aspiring Station made us very welcome, fed us with hot scones and later we returned there for a very pleasant buffet chicken dinner with half a dozen other stalkers. Two or three of the hunters were Americans—Dale Williams of the Williams Gunsight Company and his offsider Kane Petersen, with New Zealand guides John Joiner and his mate Malcolm. The Americans had been allocated the headwaters of the East Branch, but as the weather for flying didn't appear very bright, we agreed they hunt near the homestead on country shown on our permit.

Doug, Russell and I had our base camp erected on the bush edge near Snowy Creek, a couple of miles up the grass flats beyond Aspinall's.

Carrying enough supplies for four or five days, the three of us were heading upriver at first light next morning. Snowy Creek was no trouble to negotiate but the East Branch of the Matukituki is a hazardous river which floods very rapidly and has few fords. We crossed at the cattle ford but even so the water was up to our thighs and not very warm. The cattle trail drifts into the trees but Russell and I soon angled to the left to check a small grass clearing.

I knew there were deer about before I reached the opening for I got a strong whiff of pungent deer odour. About 200 yards away across the river we had recently crossed, half a mile downstream, five hinds grazed blissfully on the short sweet pasture. We watched them a moment or two, but as there was no stag about I gave a roar. Response was immediate. From the shadows a big stag leapt to his feet and stood gazing directly in our direction. I swung the binoculars on to him. Long brow points and treys, but no bay points, though there appeared to be a fine bunch of top tines. They were hard to evaluate as a birch branch was tangled in one antler. Pitching the rucksack to the ground I sprawled the rifle across it, centred on his chest and squeezed off. The heavy stag spun and fled into the birches.

"You've missed him!" exclaimed Russell, horrified.

"No! Shooting target at Dannevirke a week ago this musket hit the spotter three times at 200 yards. It's bang on the button."

A little rashly I forecast: "That stag is lying dead fifty yards in the bush. With a straight-on chest shot a stag seldom falls immediately."

We went to investigate but the surging East Branch, deep and swift, made crossing impossible. Promising ourselves we would circle back from base camp on our return and search, we headed on upstream.

But I never did get back to find him. Three days later I was even more certain I had killed the stag for, passing at dawn with fresh supplies, I saw the five hinds again in exactly the same meadow, now squired by a young, proud spiker. The spiker wouldn't be around if the big stag was alive.

Our trip ended in a tremendous flood, with even Snowy Creek barring our way ten feet deep, but young William Aspinall later went to search and found the stag—a ten-pointer.

An hour's tramp up through the birches along the river brought us out to a small pleasant clearing known as Kitchener Flat. The grass was lush and long, suggesting few deer nearby. A little further on we came on a casual hunter's overnight camp, gear discarded near his horse while he made a morning stalk. The hunter was Dave, an employee of Aspinall's, hunting venison during the weekend.

Kitchener Creek, draining the south-eastern wall of 10,000-foot Mt Aspiring, tumbles down to join the East Branch at the clearing. An hour and a half upstream from the Forks, heavily-forested Kitchener Valley opens out to a wide shingle and grass flat of its own with a rock campsite somewhere in the birches at the far end.

Doug Johnston tramped up to stalk the Aspiring Flats, as the clearing in the Kitchener Stream is called, while Russell and I dumped our packs and climbed high into the snowgrass to the east, up towards the Albert Burn tops. We were soon clear of the bush, miles of glorious snowgrass ahead, but the whole ridge was quite devoid of game except for one bruised eight-pointer Russell stalked with his camera.

To the south a wide bush gully, gashed by an ugly chasm, divided us from a fine snowgrass slope above the East Branch. As usual all the deer were across the chasm and quite inaccessible. Several stags were roaring, holding a few hinds on the bush edge, and one great stag, which seemed to carry a cluster of tops, held at least fifteen hinds that we could count with the binoculars.

Splitting occasionally to cover more ground, Russell and I climbed almost to the snowgrass saddle leading into the Albert Burn watershed. The day was glorious with an excellent view of Mt Aspiring, Rob Roy, and other great peaks to the west. We used up a considerable amount of film, for my mate and I both carried two cameras each.

Russell took a shorter, better route descending through the beech forest toward evening and had already collected his pack from beside the river by the time I got there. Though he had been gone only a short while a spiker was already hungrily sampling the damp grass. Doubting that Doug had shot meat, for we had heard no gunfire, I took a careful bead on the young stag's shoulder and dropped it. I was surprised to find the bullet had struck high in the neck and, though I didn't know it then, the ten-pointer stag shot near base camp had also been hit far too high.

Russell and I reached the leaning rock camp well after dark, stumbling along an unfamiliar and overgrown trail through the bush. Stags were roaring like bulls all around us in the darkness—how close was hard to tell—but the entrancing sound certainly helps to carry a heavy pack.

Doug had a cheerful fire reflecting from the granite, which helped Russell and me to locate the camp. There was room to sleep half a dozen men stretched among the boulders in the shelter of a huge rock, some sixty feet long and shelving out twenty feet or more. Earlier stalkers had left a few utensils and an old ten-pointer's antlers.

We were again away before sun-up. Doug went upstream to climb near the lovely waterfall higher up the valley. Russell crossed to stalk Rainbow Creek, a tributary of the Kitchener, while I headed back down the mile-long flat. With the wind in my favour I skirted the birches, but the only deer seen was a lonely eight-pointer mooching across the valley.

I climbed high into the birches and within a couple of hours found a deer track which led me out to the scrubby ledge where I shot the chamois as already described.

Determined to search the tussock tops after having climbed so far, I battled into the storm. Fresh deer sign was negligible though old tracks seemed to indicate the deer wintered on this northern slope. The face was very steep, dotted with bluffs and ribbed with dark, sheer chasms. I noted a fresh deer track or two as I struggled miserably on to a bluff. Blizzard conditions prevailed, snow and sleet slashing at my parka, and I was shivering violently.

Again I smelt the stag before I saw him. The animal roared just below, then came charging out of a hollow following a reluctant hind. It was an ugly, malformed beast, with six points on one antler, but only a short forked tine on the right antler.

The deer were soon alerted by a hind dashing down from somewhere above. I hadn't seen her in the drifting rain clouds. I watched them go, then followed down, as camp lay somewhere directly below. Scrambling down through some rather hazardous bluffs, I came on the herd of deer huddling miserably together. They fled for miles, way back along the face I had come. I soon found out why. They had nowhere else to go to escape. The snowgrass fell away in a fearful cliff with the trees waving far below.

I retreated into the storm, scrambling back the way I had come earlier. An hour later I came on the stag for the third time. He had finally calmed down and lay down in shelter with his harem, quite close to where I had shot the chamois. Remembering how poor my shooting had been I determined to test its accuracy on the malformed stag, for his progeny wouldn't enrich any trophy room.

Where the first carefully aimed bullet went, I don't know—high I believe—but I emptied the rifle at him, crammed more shells in and finally brought old one-horn down in a blaze of gunsmoke. I was absolutely disgusted with my 30.06 and detached the scope sight, dropping it into my rucksack. There was one lone cartridge left to hunt my way down through the bush to camp.

Both my companions had been thawing around the campfire for several hours. Russell had stalked a big ten-pointer in the bush and left him to grow, and Doug had sneaked up to a roaring six-pointer.

It rained steadily well into the night and the rock above developed several steady leaks where water was seeping through the faults. Toward dusk Russell turned out a reasonable line of damper scones, cooked in the frypan.

Clouds were low with light drizzle next morning. Doug decided to stalk the ten-pointer Russell had seen, while Russell was going to stalk high above Aspiring clearing to look for a chamois.

I tramped three or four miles away back down to the East Branch and the Kitchener Flat clearing to test-fire my 30.06. I could have shot it near camp of course, but I hate stirring stalking ground with gunfire, and it would have ruined Doug and Russell's morning hunt too.

Deer had brushed the dew-laden grass on Kitchener Flat but none were in sight. It didn't take long to check and alter the scope. The bullets were landing much too high, lifting the sand a foot or fifteen inches above the rocks aimed at. A drastic alteration in elevation and in half a dozen shots I was right on the target again, splitting asunder very satisfactorily the last couple of stones at 200 long strides across the river shingle.

We should check our rifles more often than we do, particularly after bouncing about in a landrover six or seven hundred miles. But strings of gunshots near civilisation aren't welcomed and when in hunting country we don't like test-shooting either. So you carry the rifle, just a bit unsure of its accuracy perhaps, until the big fellow gets away.

With renewed confidence in my rifle, I slung it across my shoulder and climbed into the mists.

The first stag aimed at died swiftly and surely, and two more big trophy beasts besides. But that's a story I'll speak of next time.

The Stags of Mt Aspiring

DEW GLISTENING ON THE GRASS, mist shrouding the valleys, stags roaring ahead.

From our camp in Kitchener Flat in the East Branch of the Matukituki I climbed steadily straight up the face for over an hour before four alarmed deer skittered across a rise. They were obviously frightened for a strong cold breeze was taking my scent in front and to the right.

The main snowgrass slopes lay ahead, and as I breasted the rise, I saw more bands of alarmed red deer trotting across far above under the bluffs, making for the bush of Chasm Creek to my left.

A hind and fawn dashed across just above, disappearing in a depression on the bush fringe. There appeared to be a likely little hollow there so I hurried across in time to see the startled fawn and its mother leap the stream and dash into the shelter birches. Poised by the trees, a huge red stag paused to glance above at the herd of seventeen deer which were streaming down a game trail above him.

In one movement my little stalking pack was flung to the ground and I dived and rested the rifle across it. The stag's great rack of antlers showed wide and high in the scope. There was no time to count points or gain breath, though I had climbed a couple of thousand feet without pause.

The tapered telescopic sight centred on his shoulder and as the bullet struck, the stag flinched and spun away. Another quick snap shot at the running stag and he collapsed. Both shots were vital shoulder hits, with a 150-grain Winchester projectile, range 200 yards. I was disappointed to find my stag carried only eleven points, as one top point just wasn't there. Length of antler was a reasonable thirty-seven inches.

Caching the antlers in a birch tree to retrieve on my return, I climbed higher to stalk the scrub slope where Russell and I had sighted a big stag and fifteen hinds three or four days earlier. But the only deer there were a hind and fawn, which I stalked and photographed.

A steep snowgrass basin lies below the high pass over the tops into Mill Creek and 700 yards above I could see another hind and fawn. Not wishing to alarm them I kept a spur between us as I climbed level, then high beyond them. Under the bluffs fresh snow lay an inch deep and higher, in the pass, it was six inches thick. Before climbing further I paused to eat a meal of cold venison steak and drink melting snow water from a tarn.

The hind and fawn were still drowsing far below when I sidled under the bluff to angle into the pass. They saw me, panicked, and decided to cross over too, climbing hurriedly straight towards me. Knowing they would alert any deer ahead, I wondered whether I should shoot one, but then the shot itself would frighten any deer in the pass. There was only one thing to do—beat the doe and fawn to the summit. The saddle must be about 6,000 feet high, but I floundered up through the soft snow at a gasping run.

A whole herd of deer was fleeing along the ridge, past a distant tarn, making for the Albert Burn Divide. I flopped in the snow, and as the stag turned to marshal his last two hinds, my 30.06 spoke once. At the gunshot the beast ran three or four steps and pitched headlong in the snow. For a moment or two the hinds milled about uncertainly, waiting for their master, then filed up over the crest. There were thirteen of them. I ran the 250 yards to look at my trophy and was disappointed again to find that it was only a pretty eleven-pointer, similar in length and spread to the other eleven, but whereas the other trophy lacked one top tine this head was minus a lower bay point.

Mill Creek is a bleak, cold snowgrass valley draining to the south-east. Jerry Aspinall grazes cattle there all summer, and winters them on the sunny western slope I had climbed ascending from the Matukituki. There was a bunch of Hereford cattle way below and the glasses picked up half a dozen deer way beyond. Curiously, with the rut at its height, all were stags. They were miles away, though I could see one stag carried only one antler—perhaps smashed off fighting or else a relative of the odd, malformed beast I had shot a few days earlier.

The commercial venison hunters with their helicopters had shot up this country a couple of months previously, and were actually well overdue back in again, so I was very lucky to see the deer I did.

I spent an hour or more on the Divide searching the nearby basins, but late in the afternoon I descended again to stalk the scrub face above Chasm Creek headwaters. There were a couple of stags roaring in the bush below, and way across—beyond some inaccessible bluffs and gorges—two or three little mobs of deer grazed in the evening sunlight.

Then from the trees below came a throaty roar and a whole herd of deer came jostling and pushing along a narrow game trail. Hinds were nose over rump, one after another, like a herd of impatient milking cows heading for the cow bail. I gasped as the great top points of a huge stag appeared above the scrub, prodding his hinds into line. The stag disappeared, then came into view 300 yards below.

Stalking closer with so many watchful hinds spreading out to feed would be extremely difficult, so I sprawled across a bush, tipped the muzzle downwards and fired. The monarch staggered, then my next swift bullet had hit him. Perhaps my third shot missed—I never checked—but my fourth bullet sent the stag sprawling.

I scrambled down and was elated to count fourteen points. The tops were heavy and numerous, four tines on one crown, five on the other. Brow and trey tines were long and curving, but unfortunately one bay tine was missing and the other woefully short. With a spread of thirty-four and a half inches and length of thirty-seven and three-quarter inches this was the largest stag I shot on Mount Aspiring. It was an old beast, possibly past its prime.

Encumbered with the eleven-pointer and fourteen-pointer, plus its cape, I struggled down another half-mile to where my first eleven of the day was hung in the beech.

The sun was low above Aspiring so I reluctantly left the fourteen in the tree and scrambled down to base with the two lighter eleven-pointers. Several little groups of deer were drifting from the beeches to graze: some trotted back to cover but others just watched curiously as I descended.

It was quite dark by the time I negotiated the bush and reached camp. Russell had shot a nice chamois, but Doug still had no trophies.

The morning was dull and toward noon steady rain set in. Russell climbed the cold snowgrass slope farther upstream and shot a fair eleven-pointer and photographed other deer. I climbed to retrieve my fourteen, while Doug, who had climbed with me, carried on the stalk to shoot and lose a stag roaring in the open birches. He searched for a couple of hours, then climbed to look into Mill Creek.

I spent the day clearing the meat from the skulls of my three trophies and fleshing the headskin. In between times I stirred a billy of stew on the fire and talked with a large party of young trampers passing upstream.

Russell was back in fair time and remarked that perhaps we

should push out to base that night. If steady rain continued the Matukituki River could be dangerous by morning. So we made a few preparations for a quick departure if Doug were agreeable. He didn't come in until dark, but had already considered shifting camp.

We were on the trail just as the last light vanished. Doug carried the only torch in the party—and that wasn't much good. It was a two-cell rubber flashlight but the perspex glass gave only a feeble glow. Russell and I each toiled with two sets of antlers atop our packs. It was a nightmare tramp. Every time I hooked a root and fell full length, the jaw and teeth of the fourteen-pointer clouted me on the back of the head. I'm not sure whether my scalp was bruised or just bitten! What had been an hour's pleasant walk in took three hours on return. It rained steadily and once we lost the track and wandered disconsolately about searching for blaze or boot marks. Antlers are bad enough to carry at any time, but in complete darkness they hooked every unseen tree. Doug's dim light always seemed to be disappearing ahead while Russell and I floundered over roots or boulders.

Wondering if the river would be rising, we each broke a stout pole from the last birch tree and strode out across the flats.

The river was a swirling flood and looked dangerous, though in pouring rain at ten o'clock at night we couldn't see much. There was a nylon rope in Russell's pack but before we could even discuss the situation Doug plunged into the flooded river. The ford was sixty or seventy yards across and soon we could hardly even see Doug struggling to stand. Russell and I were appalled. With a rope, someone might get swept off his feet and soaked but not come to too much harm; or the three of us could brace each other crossing together on a pole. If the river was really too deep we could always make an uncomfortable camp where we were.

With some reluctance Russell and I waded in, for we could hardly let Doug cross entirely alone. The flood was up to our crutch, then churning waist-deep, surging over the boulders. It was really dangerous, and a slip would have been fatal. All my weight was on the birch pole as I braced against the torrent, inching my boots slowly forward over the big boulders under foot. Once my rifle slipped down my arm, scope sight dipping in the freezing river. I could barely stand against the tugging, swirling flood, but somehow I made a grab for the weapon and hung it dangling around my neck. At least it couldn't tangle in my legs and trip me, though I knew if I went down I'd be in real trouble.

Somehow we made it, floundering the last few yards from the river, my mates and I angled right to cross Snowy Creek to base. The rain was teeming down, but we couldn't get any wetter anyway.

All that night and next day the downpour continued. Shallow Snowy Creek was a raging terror 10 feet deep, the East Matukituki a swollen flooded giant, sprawling across the river flats, halting all travel.

Even our base camp was rather cramped and damp. We had brought a spacious 10 x 14 tent, complete with poles, but mislaid all the guy ropes. So there the three of us were stuck, in a small leaking 8 x 8 centre pole tent, crammed with soaked gear.

Eventually the flooded Matukituki subsided, then away, off to Stewart Island.

South to Stalk Stewart Island

THE FISHING CRAFT eased into the long swell as we headed along the coast; Port Adventure, Chew Tobacco Bay, Christmas Village, Yankee River, Long Harry—odd and picturesque were the names of the various bays and beaches. Christened by the sealers and whalers over a century earlier, by now no one knows who Long Harry was, or how "Chew Tobacco" came by that remarkable name.

Jimmie Ballantyne, our skipper, was broadly built and easygoing. He remarked that he would have to go round to Ruggedy Bay fairly soon.

"One of the boats dropped off a couple of hunters there three weeks ago. They wanted to stay about six or seven days but I just haven't got back yet. By now those boys should be really pleased to see me."

When Doug and I watched the *Mavis* sail away, I felt just like the original Robinson Crusoe cast up on the beach.

Landing had had its moments too. There was a tiny beach below our campsite so, instead of landing on the rocks, Jimmie dumped us on the sand. Doug jumped from the dinghy, but a following wave lifted the boat right over my mate and he came out of the surf looking like a drowned spaniel.

Doug Johnston knew our block well: he had stalked it the last three consecutive seasons and taken a fine whitetail on his first trip. The campsite was some 200 feet above the beach, in the edge of low forest. The steep, sandy slope down to the water fascinated me, for wind and wave had recently lifted some of the brush and rushes, exposing half a dozen crumbling Maori middens of long, long ago. Among the burnt stones were bird and fish bones, half a dozen types of sea shell, and a few broken stone tools. I picked up a couple of interesting bones too, one split for the marrow, which appeared to date from either a cannibal or moa feast. Later Doug picked up a fine stone axe a mile or two east in the forest.

Before chopping poles and generally making a commotion setting up camp, Doug and I stalked a low scrubby point jutting half a mile out to sea. Muddy penguin trails led up a steep bank from the sea to their shore homes in dense, unpalatable green fern. We saw one or two in the bush, but heard them more frequently. Doug and I pushed along the penguin trails on to the headland, but parted to drive the point. But if a big whitetail buck was there we saw no sign of him. Way out on the headland where the granite cliffs plunged a sheer 200 feet into the southern ocean, I shot a red deer hind for meat, and in an hour we were back at the campsite.

Toward evening I stalked a bush spur above the sea while Doug hunted the hill behind camp. Just across the creek, the Forest Service had strung up a barbed wire enclosure to check forest regeneration, but the wire itself was poor and so was their fencing, for the deer kept the vegetation close-cropped inside the enclosure too.

I saw my first whitetail deer close by—a doe, standing forty yards off in the bush. I watched her until she took alarm and leapt gracefully away. The whitetails don't crash through the scrub like a red does, but spring nimbly over the bushes. Soon another whitetail doe peered inquisitively past a birch and a third darted across my path. Somewhere in the heavy bush to the left, a red stag roared furiously, and from the ridge ahead another stag answered the challenge.

On my first hunt for a trophy whitetail I wasn't in the least interested in red deer, but came on the stag ahead somewhat sooner than I had expected. He was bellowing like a bull in fairly open scrubby bush. I saw a hind first, and edging away from her, found myself right on two more hinds. They sensed my presence and tensed to run, but waited for the stag. He roared again, not a bit agitated, hidden by a tangled mat of hanging supplejack vine. I felt the breeze changing and the stag charged away in panic, a black-antlered eight-pointer.

Further on I alarmed another whitetail doe, and toward dusk I swung inland to circle back to camp. I had heard of course that whitetail don't venture far inland, but the idea seemed so odd I hardly took it seriously. But it's a fact! The whitetail loves the sea coast, and 400 yards from the waves whitetail tracks and sign virtually disappear. The bush doesn't appear any different—it's all quite open with many rimu trees. Whitetail favour the supplejack thickets and trim the vines as high as they can reach. They also relish a tiny, bright green, grass-like plant which covers the ground wherever the sun breaches the trees.

Quite surprised to leave the whitetail area so abruptly, I hurried through the trees, but swung aside as the other red stag roared in the valley below. Again I saw the hinds first, then the stag (another eight-pointer) came charging proudly up through the birches.

Next morning Doug suggested we traverse four or five miles of bush to visit Sandfly Bay. That isn't the name of the locality, but Jimmie Ballantyne specifically requested me not to define exact areas since from then on everyone would want to go there. Personally I'd say the chances of a trophy don't depend too greatly on locality, for the fishermen occasionally see bucks on every beach, and 95 per cent of the hunting is bush stalking anyway.

One stalker I met believed whitetails were more plentiful but smaller on the south-east coast below Half Moon Bay. There are not so many whitetail anywhere along the western coast in the Mason Bay area, but many more reds.

This old shelter in the Mararoa bush is known as "Igly". Built of round birch poles and with no door, it proved a bit draughty.

Carried in by packhorse, this tiny shanty lies hidden far up the Whitestone. Note how the rifle almost dwarfs the door opening.

At our camp on Kitchener clearing up the east Matukituki. Doug Johnston dries out after a wet night.

This fine buck chamois was shot on the slopes of Mt Aspiring.

Stewart Island is roughly triangular in shape, with one side to the south-east, another forty-odd miles facing the north-east, and a rugged fifty-mile coast on the west. Almost all the island is heavily wooded and the highest point, Mount Anglem, is only just over 3,000 feet.

Years ago, Government deer cullers hunted Stewart Island intensively, but by now the only sign of their activities is an occasional blaze mark or axe-scarred log. Doug led the way along an old, tortuous, culler's trail, but the bush was so open we would have done better to pick our own route. Once a red stag roared ahead and I kept the stag's attention by roaring vociferously while Doug sneaked closer. The stag was only a six-pointer. Further on we swung down to the coast to stalk a scrubby, partly-open area, the only such place for miles. White-tail sign there was much more prominent, and it seemed clear that the little deer favoured any clearing.

Striking into the bush again I was leading when I realised Doug had disappeared. Rather disconcerted I waited for a while, then roared half a dozen times to let him know my whereabouts. Doug didn't appear for quite a while, but an excited little four-point red stag came running. It was amusing to see his surprise and reluctance to believe his eyes. The stag would watch, leap away, then quietly circle to eye me again from the trees.

The coast was rugged and picturesque. We scrambled down to the shore, followed it for some time, then had to climb the cliffs again before finally Sandfly Bay was reached about 1 pm. It was a lovely beach, two miles of golden sand, packed high into dunes like the sand sea of the Sahara. There was no sign of red deer—we were beyond their territory—but whitetail tracks criss-crossed the virgin sands.

Doug agreed that Sandfly Bay seemed well worth hunting, and suggested that we make tracks straight back to base camp and bring a tent and sleeping bags.

"But that means we'll spend half a day tramping each way and arrive back right where we are here this time tomorrow. Let's stay and hunt right now. We can shoot a deer and eat that and sleep around a fire."

"We haven't even any tea or salt," Doug remarked, but he agreed to my plan.

Doug climbed to hunt the rimu terraces running inland above

"Sandfly" River, while I stalked an extensive forest basin beyond the beach. At each high tide the sea builds up a sand bar across the Sandfly River mouth and the stream spreads back through a maze of backwaters, sluggish lagoons and meandering streams. I climbed a low spur, found myself in a tangle of supplejack vines, and edged south to the bank of a deep, barely moving stream. Rotting vegetation in the slow-moving water gave a pleasantly distinctive, smoky colour and flavour.

In midstream a graceful toe-toe bush brushed its fronds in the water and a shaft of sunlight lit the brown depths, making a lovely picture. Doug used an 8 mm movie camera, but I preferred to handle a pair of 35 mm cameras, one for colour and one for black and white. Getting the picture angle just right—one arm hooked around a leaning punga—I was hanging precariously out over deep water when the camera triggered with a sharp click.

I nearly fell in the drink as a startled whitetail leapt through the bushes on the opposite shore, not twenty-five feet distant. The deer paused, partly screened by a manuka bush. I recovered my balance, eased the camera to the leaves and groped for the .243.

As the scope sight centred on the branches I wondered briefly if the light, little, high-velocity bullet would smash through to the deer. Boom! The shot rang out and the deer lurched away. I had to search 100 yards to find a ford, and then I discovered that the river had forked and I had to wade another tributary. Whitetail take readily to water and I chose a well-marked deer crossing as probably the best route.

In luxuriant fern a whitetail doe hunched miserably. My rifle sprang up to administer the coup-de-grâce, but when I examined the deer I was surprised to find this was another doe and not the one I had fired at earlier. A careful search showed one or two blood stains and I soon found the first carcass.

I had an impression that the first deer fired at was a buck, but I was mistaken—both deer were plump whitetail does, the first whitetail deer I had shot. Anyway, we had agreed to shoot the first deer for meat and the skins themselves would make an interesting addition to the trophy room.

Wandering through the swampy rainforest, wading and leaping the maze of streams, I started to wonder after a couple of hours when I would reach dry ground again. One whitetail doe darted from close by, but a flash of white-tailed "flag" was all I glimpsed as she disappeared in the neck-high, coarse fern undergrowth.

Late in the evening I reached a wide area of undulating sand-dunes rippled by sea breezes, but the only signs of deer were wandering footprints. Whitetail deer are supposed to favour seaweed to eat but I saw nothing to endorse the idea. They certainly roamed the beaches, but nowhere did the deer tracks lead toward any of the numerous piles of seaweed cast up by the tide.

The sunset was spectacular and must have been engineered by Kodak. The beach was a couple of miles long and in the dusk I could see Doug's campfire from way back. He had a cheerful blaze, but I suggested that by morning the damp dew would be rather chilly.

I had earlier picked out a sheltered possie in the bush edge, so we dragged in a few more dead branches for firewood, then smashed down enough leafy manuka branches to fashion a bivvy.

I planted a pole into a steep, dry bark, tied it with flax to a handy sapling, and we laid the manuka brush to make a tent-like shelter. With the fire in front and a whitetail skin each to sleep on, we soon had quite a comfortable camp. Doug had even found a seat of sorts—a banana case flotsam from the waves.

We yarned awhile and cooked our tea grilling venison on a pointed stick over the manuka coals.

Without waiting to build up the fire, we quietly left camp at dawn to stalk the open beach, but saw no deer though several animals had crossed my boot trail during the night. The most amazing thing was their curiosity. Doug's fire on the beach, thirty yards from our bivvy and other fire, had attracted at least half a dozen deer. Their hoof marks had scattered the warm ash, and they must have stood in the shadows and watched us.

We cooked more steak for breakfast and also a generous slice each to carry for lunch. After all, we had nothing else to eat, but that didn't worry me—I can go further and faster on raw, red meat than any food I know.

The only thing about our bivvy camp that didn't seem right was the fact that the mosquitoes feasted on me. I was covered in itchy lumps and lean, tough, grizzled old Doug Johnston had never a bite!

Doug and I parted at the Sandfly River to stalk the bush to base camp. My companion would take the higher terraces while I hunted the shoreline. Doug came on a whitetail doe and her fawn in the birches, filmed them, and went his way, and still the two deer just watched him. Far more curious than afraid, they could never have seen a man before. Most whitetails are away very quickly though, alert and quick.

I saw no deer until I worked out to stalk a rather open scrubby point. Rocky knobs are a feature of the Stewart Island bush and as I was stepping lightly past a granite pile I saw a whitetail slipping over the crest. Remembering there was a small, damp opening beyond the bluff, I turned and sprinted back the way I had come.

I beat the buck! With an eye behind him the handsome creature stepped warily along the narrow trail between bluff and sea, then halted abruptly as he realised I was ahead. The only cover was a dense manuka bush and his whole body melted behind it, motionless. The scope sight showed the deer's outline, but when the .243 spoke the buck sprang back, darting once more into the mass of boulders. I searched and tracked, then finally returned to the starting point and found the fresh bullet scar in a tree trunk. A wisp of deer hair lay by the torn bark. Then one spot of blood, yards on—another. It took me another hour to find the deer buck, hidden under a bush 100 yards away.

He was a beautiful animal, large and in excellent condition, but antler growth was poor—only the horns curving up and forward with no branching tines. I tried to reach base by boulder-jumping and cliff-climbing along under the bluffs on the seashore, but in-rushing waves in a narrow, deep cleft defeated me. Geology is another of my interests and I filled my pockets with colourful rock specimens. Caves scar the cliffs and the endless rush of tides had polished the pebbles.

Sunrise was a colourful sight, but Jimmie Ballantyne's little fishing boat rode anchored in our bay, wallowing in a rising sea.

"Don't like the look of that!" said Doug. "Jimmie's here to take us off."

"But we've only just got here. We shouldn't go out for another three or four days."

But that was the way it was. A bad storm warning was out and Jimmie stated that he mightn't be able to get back to our remote beach for two or three weeks. Later that morning, in steady rain, we dismantled the tent and trudged down to the beach.

Embarkation was quite exciting. Seas now pounded the beach, so Jimmie rowed his dinghy close to a massive ragged rock. The swells whirled, came rolling on, splashed over our rock, then as they poured out again Doug or myself would leap down to a slippery exposed rock by deep water. Jimmie would edge smoothly in and one pack, or a rifle, or tent, would be pitched into the little boat. Action was swift and perilous. As the rifle or pack hit the planks, Jimmie would be heaving on the oars again, dragging the dinghy out to avoid the great seas tossing him on to the rocks while we would leap back up the rock. The rollers would surge six to eight feet deep over our landing, splashing through and on to the cliffs. There would be a wild surge of foam and receding waves, then down Doug would scramble with another bundle of gear before the next wave hit.

The Hunters of Half Moon

PACK, PARKA AND RIFLE, that is standard afternoon dress on the main street of Stewart Island's only village. After all, where else in New Zealand would deer regularly wander the streets and be shot occasionally on the football ground?

Sprightly Miss Prentice, in her bush-surrounded home, complained that a cheeky whitetail deer kept nibbling her choice bulbs. I didn't see any deer there, but a complacent weka paraded on the lawn.

Another resident remarked that when her husband patrolled the vegetable garden with a rifle at dawn or sunset, he never saw a deer, but at lunchtime the previous day she needed a carrot and a sleek whitetail doe was sampling the other end of the row "and didn't want to go!"

One wet Monday night, a week after Easter, Alvin Hicks, a

helpful Stewart Island fisherman, flashed his torch down a muddy game trail leading into the sombre bush.

"A big whitetail buck uses this track every morning. Just on dawn I've seen him cross here when I'm going down to the boat."

Another flick of the torch.

"See those two old cars? The buck was standing between them yesterday. Trouble is to get a shot at him with all these houses around."

I guess we weren't more than 400 yards from Half Moon's post office and wharves, but the whitetail is a deer that can live and thrive close to people. The species do so in America and also in Stewart Island.

For some odd reason, New Zealand's whitetail deer are often called "Virginian deer". Possibly our liberations originated from that State in America, but the term "Virginia deer" is a purely New Zealand name for a species widespread through eastern USA and Canada. Apart from Stewart Island the only other New Zealand herd of whitetail deer is a small herd around the Dart Valley at the head of Lake Wakatipu.

In 1968 the best whitetail trophy for the year was shot within a few miles of Half Moon Bay by a keen visiting stalker camped in town with his family. Who knows, perhaps Doug and I left the best hunting ground behind when we headed north to stalk whitetail. Mind you, there's lots of bush and cover right into town and the population isn't large, only about 500 people, mostly fishermen or retired folk.

Half Moon Bay, or Oban as it is named on the maps, has a pub and a post office, a couple of stores and a very fine museum. There is no chemist or doctor, not even a taxi. With no public electric power, most permanent residents run their own diesel plants. Few people own a car as the roads disappear into bush tracks within half a mile.

Nearly every day during the summer and twice a week during winter, the ferry boat *Wairua* runs across the turbulent Foveaux Strait from Bluff in Southland. An amphibian plane is scheduled to call twice a week too, but is available for emergency at $24 a flight across to Invercargill.

Many Southland people spend their holidays at Stewart Island and have built baches in the bush ("cribs" they're called down south) and Doug Johnston and I were soon installed in one. It served as a base to stow gear and camp while waiting to go in or out by fishing craft to our rather remote and stormbound hunting block.

The *Wairua* leaves Bluff at 8 am and is berthed at Half Moon a little after ten o'clock, so as Jimmie Ballantyne, our fishing skipper, wasn't available that day, Doug and I picked up our rifles after lunch and did a stroll up a bush track along the shore to long-abandoned Ryan's Mill, then over the hill and down the Fern Tree Gully road to town. We saw a few tracks of whitetail and red deer, and the rather ancient paunches of three deer which had been shot and removed. Stewart Island red deer don't have a high trophy reputation, but later I inspected a very pretty fourteen-pointer shot in Fern Tree Gully a fortnight before.

We covered six or seven miles, and met only one other hunter camping by the roadside. He remarked that we were the eighth party of men with rifles to pass within an hour, but it was the last day of Easter, so that wasn't surprising.

Doug and I had our trip away hunting with skipper Jimmie Ballantyne, as described in the previous chapter, but due to an approaching storm we found ourselves cast back in Half Moon Bay earlier than intended.

With over two days in hand we debated whether to tramp across the island to Mason Bay, but it was reputed to be a long seven-hour walk each way. Doug, a seasoned tramper, was keen, but as the chance of a trophy on the trail was virtually nil, I wasn't too enthusiastic. I suppose I'm a hunter first, last and all the time, so I jumped at an offer by Roy Traill, ex-ranger of Stewart Island, to take us in to his bush camp for a few days. Next morning we tossed our packs and rifles aboard his fishing craft and chugged up Paterson Inlet for an hour or so before Roy anchored and rowed us ashore.

Roy Traill owns a lovely bush-covered peninsula rich with tall rimu. We tramped a mile or so through the forest to his camp. Many years ago, some of the adjacent property had been milled, but regrowth is now thirty or forty feet high, and thousands of healthy young rimus are thrusting toward the sunlight.

Doug and I parted and spent a couple of pleasant hours in the evening stalking the open forest. Deer had once been much more plentiful but the game trails are well grown over and many shrubs favoured by deer stand three or four feet tall, quite unmolested.

There had been a few reds through months before, judging by the dried, crumbling droppings. Only on one high knob did I find fresh sign of a whitetail deer or two. Returning at sunset along the damp sands, I discovered where the little deer had descended and wandered ahead of me. Doug sighted one fleeting whitetail in dense manuka the first evening, but failed to sight any game next morning. Neither did I.

Later we packed and walked back to the launch. Paterson Inlet is a sheltered harbour, dotted with small islets, ribbed with capes and tiny bays. Everywhere the waves lap the bush. Roy swung his craft close to the rocks so Doug and I could photograph the shags, impressive birds of three or four species and colours, eyeing us disdainfully.

At a sheltered beach of golden sand, a lovely spot for a picnic or campsite, Roy Traill swung inshore so Doug and I could hunt for an hour.

Fresh whitetail tracks wandered the shore, and as soon as I entered the bush I could see that a tiny band of these creatures lived in the area. I climbed steeply to the long point which jutted into the bay and crept quietly through the trees, swinging aside to avoid the tangle of supplejack vines which guard every hollow. Where a twisted old beech had fallen, the sunlight filtered down to encourage a stand of dense green growth—a plant I have never noted elsewhere, which carpets the ground an inch deep in favourable conditions of the Island. The whitetail love this growth, and so do the opossums, for Doug saw one grazing it in daylight.

As I stepped past the beech stump I wasn't surprised to see a whitetail deer walk towards me past the next rimu, then halt abruptly. This young spiker buck was no trophy beast but I had already spared a dozen such dainty creatures up north. The last minutes of our final hunting hour had already ticked away and this young stag would make delicious venison!

The .243 swung up and fired. I gutted the little whitetail, swung the whole carcass on to my shoulders and crashed into the supplejack, back to the launch, Half Moon Bay—and home.

PART IV
THE BIG STAGS OF FIORDLAND

Call of the Canyon

JOE'S RIVER, south-east of Milford, carries an evil reputation. The first white men through there were explorers Grave and Talbot in 1906. Not another party is known to have trod the remote Joe's River for another fifty-odd years until, in 1957, two trampers made the traverse up Joe's River, over the fearful Marshall Pass and down the North Clinton. It is real tiger country. There could be a real old man stag in there by now, or a lost wapiti bull, or maybe the last of the Morioris or even the moa.

The Joe has intrigued me for years. In 1961 I actually obtained a permit to hunt Joe's River, and intended taking American friends Lloyd Tillett and Bob Kelsey there. But on second thoughts I cancelled the block, figuring that the unexplored rainforests of Fiordland were no place for two lean cattlemen from the desert.

Nineteen sixty-eight was going to be the year I didn't head south, but that was a silly resolution. By March, Tiki, my pet red stag, was roaring spasmodically in our adjacent deer park and I started wondering aloud about the wapiti prospects. Ruth, my wife, said emphatically: "Look, I can't stand you around the place during the roaring season. Go on, get out of here!"

A fortnight later Wilby Oliver and I were travelling south, the mountains of Fiordland in view as we swung into Te Anau township.

A year or two previously I had casually met Stuart stalking up the Whitestone, at the back of Mararoa. Wilby and I happened to meet him on this occasion and Stuart insisted we spend the night in Te Anau with him.

"You and Wilby stay in my bach, sort out your gear and leave the car in our yard. How are you getting up the lake, by the

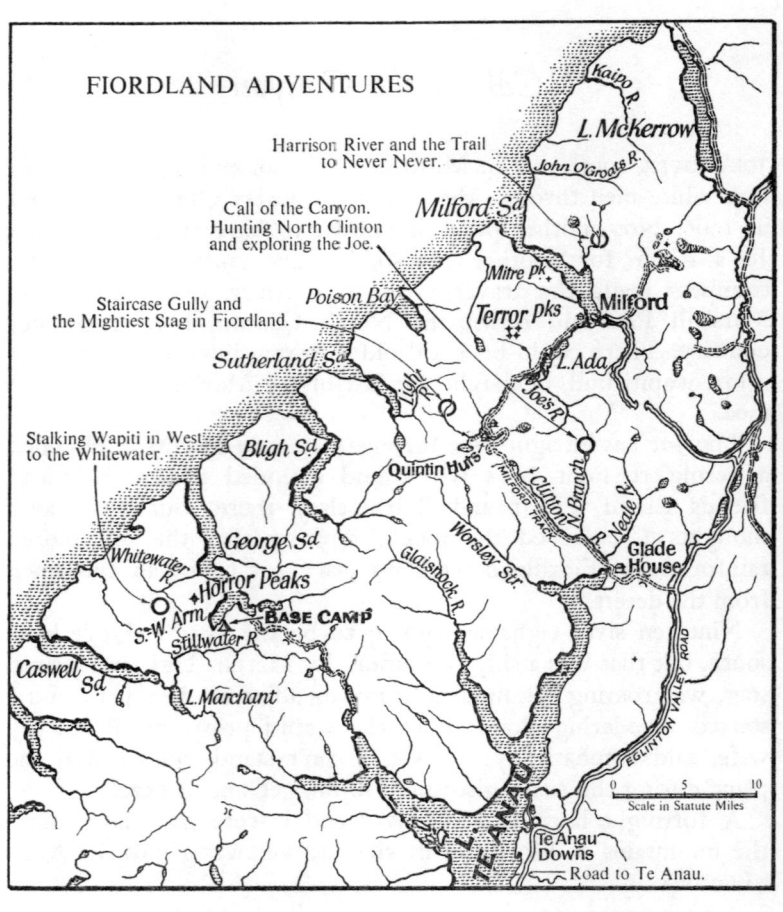

way? I'll ring Terry, my boss, and see if he will run you up in his jet."

Stuart and Terry Milligan run Te Anau Transport, and an hour before dawn next morning Stuart had cooked us a fine breakfast and Wilby and I were pounding up the tarseal toward Te Anau Downs with Terry, his jetboat trailing behind. We launched the craft in darkness and roared up the still silent lake toward Glade House. It's twenty-four miles from Te Anau Downs to the head of Lake Te Anau and the Glade House landing. Terry Milligan had us there in an hour or so, and by 8 am we were ashore and swatting sandflies. A wave and the genial transport operator was away again, jet waves fanning out from the racing craft. You know, Wilby and I had never met Terry until five o'clock that morning, yet he wouldn't even accept petrol money from us.

Wilby and I checked in at Glade House as we passed, then crossed the swaying bridge over the Clinton and started up the Milford Track. A mile or so along we met an elderly stalker walking down the trail. It was sixty-eight-year-old Bill Foley from Taihape. Bill had just seen off his party into the Neale Burn, having sadly decided that his ageing heart wasn't up to packing in.

"Wonder if I could hire a helicopter in Te Anau to land me up the Neale Burn and catch the boys," mused the Taihape hunter. Bill was still as keen as ever.

The Clinton is a lovely river, exceptionally clear and occasionally we noticed a rainbow trout or two idling in the current. A pair of blue mountain ducks squatted on the farther shore and two colourful paradise ducks squawked nearby. There was even a grey heron winging down-river; these slender birds are by no means so rare as they used to be.

It is very pleasant walking on the Milford Track, but Wilby and I found the mile pegs quite a way apart. Frankly, we were carrying too heavy a load each. Put on the scales, our packs topped sixty pounds apiece and we had another twenty pounds each of rifles, cameras and binoculars dangling around our necks. A sixty-pound load is comfortable, eighty is a drag, but we were packing in for a fourteen-day trip and tents, billies, sleeping bags, mountain stoves, fuel and food all weigh up.

Four miles upstream from Glade House the Clinton River forks, the Milford Track following the western branch. Here we swung aside into the canyon of the north branch of the Clinton. Just as we left the Milford Track three young men, two of them from Australia, came strolling along carrying a rod apiece. They told us they had just completed a ten-day hunt in fine weather up the North Clinton valley, had heard no roars and seen no deer, except numerous hinds.

The main stream of the Clinton runs very deep along much of the Milford Track but by the fork fans out to a delightful place of small grass clearings and wooded islands among the birch forest. Fords were numerous and shallow and we splashed across to the eastern bank, and trudged on upstream.

The first long pool above the shallows was 100 yards long, six or eight feet deep and held a dozen or more lounging trout. They spied us easily in the gin-clear water, and gave Wilby and me a distrustful glare before gliding off to rise lazily near the far bank. The deer have tramped out a well-defined trail along the eastern bank of the North Clinton, weaving through the boulders and tall trees.

All day the weather had been deteriorating, rain clouds building up ahead, and by 1.30 steady rain had set in. The damp bush of Fiordland does not provide many good campsites and we were somewhat surprised to sight an old decrepit, abandoned tent camp, apparently built but little used by deer cullers.

The tent itself was shot-gunned with mildew holes, but the sagging fly was still rainproof. A chimney of split birch slab had collapsed and so did the bunks when we sat on them. But they were dry, so we stayed awhile, and had a meal. The rain still teemed down so we shored up the bunks with firewood and stayed the night. Sleeping on the woodheap was quite a contrast to Stuart's comfortable bunks in Te Anau the previous night. Around 8 pm I hurried out into the rain and set out the empty billy as a rain gauge.

Next morning the rain was easing. The billy held five inches of rain and the Clinton was in churning flood. We tramped upstream, detouring back into the trees in swampy places where the flooded river had backed up the creeks.

A few miles beyond the old cullers' camp a lively stream plunges down from a hanging valley east of the Clinton. Don Cummings of Nelson, who had last been in this side valley in

1960, told me he saw the first deer ever to reach there. It was a red spiker. Don and his party christened the pleasant little valley Lily Creek, from the profusion of lovely Mt Cook lilies, and so it now appears on the map. Don had seen a very promising eleven-point wapiti in the pass beyond Lily Creek, and as Lily Creek is adjacent to Surprise Creek, an unknown branch of The Joe, that's why Wilby and I were heading up the Clinton.

Joe's River drains west into Lake Ada, near Milford Sound, and access across there is uncertain; so my mate and I had decided to have a look up the North Clinton and Lily Creek to try and reach the Joe over the high pass.

We cached an extra can of gas fuel for the mountain stove and the fishing rod in the roots of a huge birch, then swung away up Lily Creek. It's a rough route climbing into Lily Valley, and we missed the track—if there was one—struggling through a maze of moraine boulders, stunted birches, and moss. High above the stream we finally cut a fairly well-used deer track which led us over a shoulder and into the hanging valley. We almost stepped on to our first deer when I came upon a muddied wallow still stirred with yellow sludge. A disturbed little six-pointer charged up the track, hooting in alarm.

Lily Valley opened out to pleasant bush with easy tramping. The next stag must have been lazing in the black fern, for he went leaping across the trail in panic. I glimpsed three short points on each crown, to make a young royal.

We came to a small pleasant clearing, covered in low koromiko scrub. There was some dwarf snowgrass up under the northern cliffs where the avalanches plunge down. Several hinds, yearlings and fawns were in sight, but no stags. Meat we needed, so I killed a fat young hind and we added another ten pounds of meat each to our load and hung more venison in a flour bag from a nearby birch. The echoing, single gunshot seemed to wake the stags, for soon half a dozen were roaring furiously up the valley ahead. That's a glorious sound!

We wandered through a splendid park of ribbonwood and lost the trail in a nasty wilderness of moraine boulders. The dense, treacherous moss conceals hidden clefts and crevices and the deer shun the moraine, detouring wide around such dangerous, difficult places. The deer seemed to be roaring only two or three hundred yards ahead, and quietness is anything but easy, crawling up a slick, wet boulder with a ninety-pound load. There wasn't the sign of a deer mark however, and finally I left Wilby with the packs while I scouted wide, and eventually found a faint deer track.

It's essential someone stays with the pack; it is surprising how hard they are to recover after you have criss-crossed and zig-zagged about in untracked bush. They tell me there is still a complete camp lost by two new chums in the bush up the Wilkin.

Daylight was fading as we scrambled over the rocks out to a delightful clearing. The rain had ceased but clouds still hung low in the pass high ahead. Slipping off our packs, we stalked hurriedly along the edge of the opening. A stag roared, then wandered aimlessly into the tussock. I hurriedly focussed the binoculars. "It's only an eight-pointer!"

The stag roared again.

"There's a hind, three—five of them—over by the far bush!" exclaimed my mate.

I saw the big stag first, stepping from the bright green ribbon-wood trees.

"Do you want him, Wilby? The stag's worth shooting. Three on each top."

"You saw him first. He's yours."

The range wasn't long. The 30.06 spoke once and the great stag collapsed instantly.

We ran out into the open, glanced about hurriedly and ran on to the fallen animal. He was an absolutely magnificent beast, sleek and very fat, with a reasonable twelve-point head, thirty-eight inches long.

One stag was still roaring valiantly high amongst the birches ahead, so we hurried on up the valley. Away to the right a cream-coloured bull was climbing steadily up to the snowgrass. Undoubtedly wapiti blood in that animal, but the antlers didn't appear exciting. It was cold and raining again.

"Have a go after that stag that's roaring," I suggested to Wilby. "I think he's in that bush across there, about half a mile away. I'll go back and pitch the tent before it's too dark."

Close to the dead stag I set up camp and trimmed extra meat from the beast.

Wilby returned having not sighted the stag, and we brewed a pot of soup while the steak sizzled. We then cooked up powdered potato and freeze-dried peas, and then topped it off with rice and dried apricots. Stags were bellowing all around, and hinds honked a warning at every flash of torch or candle. Soon after darkness a tremendous avalanche thundered into the valley, and around 8 pm there was a prolonged earthquake. The birds were calling too, morepork quite close by and wekas and keas by the camp.

By midnight we were awake again, with a stag bellowing furiously close to the tent. In the still cold air we could hear him draw in a breath, then expel another thunderous bellow.

Usually Wilby and I breakfast well before daybreak, but the stags were still roaring so close by we didn't wish to frighten them with the lighted tent, so lay quietly in our bags until shooting light. Wilby checked the load in his rifle, and crawled out of the pup tent. There were no deer in sight so Wilby crept toward the nearest birches. I sidled down the clearing to watch beyond the trees. The stag roared again several times before I spotted him. He was now half a mile away, just above the bush in dense scrub below the southern canyon wall. A curtain of rock half-enclosed him and formed a natural sound shell which hurled his roar in a remarkable manner. The big binoculars showed only seven points.

Wilby cooked up a goulash of last night's rice mixed with porridge for breakfast, while I fried steak to carry for lunch.

Beyond the clearing there was still extensive birch bush, rising to snowgrass ringed by the cirque and cliff walls. Occasionally the clouds parted a little, with a glimpse of tremendous snow-capped mountains thrusting far above us.

We followed the deer trail taken by the wapiti bull the previous evening but never saw the animal again. There was one lone wapiti cow high across the valley up under the cliffs. The stag for which Wilby had unsuccessfully tried the previous night was still challenging, standing on a steep slope half a mile beyond the birches. Eight or nine hinds were scattered wide about him. Some stags corral their harem viciously and use their sharp horns freely to chastise any wandering hinds.

This stag let his hinds wander freely while he stood on a prominent rock and roared. We studied the stag closely from across the valley but the antlers definitely appeared to be lacking their bay tines.

"Probably a ten with three on each top," pronounced Wilby.

"Let's go right to the head of the valley and see if there's anything better."

We saw several little groups of deer, hinds and fawns, and a disconsolate and lonely six-pointer, but nothing exciting. High above us, four or five deer became agitated and climbed high into the bluffs. It was absolutely sheer for 1,000, maybe 3,000 feet above, high into the clouds, and the deer panicked when scrambling across a very nasty bluff and nearly fell. Their terror wasn't pleasant and we were distinctly pleased to see them scrabble up over the rim into the pass.

Neither Wilby nor I were enthralled by the route up the cliffs to the pass which led out above Surprise Creek and the Joe. A waterfall plunged six or eight hundred feet, and on the steep, smooth rock face to the right I could trace out a seldom-used deer trail. Slinging our rifles to give us two hands to hold by, we climbed steadily four or five hundred feet before coming to a nasty steep spot where the desperate deer had scrabbled loose moss from the rocks.

"Now where do you go?" queried Wilby.

"Well, if we grab that tussock there, and it holds, then reach that little bush, we should make it to the ledge. There's a bad bit higher up, but then we should be able to angle back to the waterfall."

Wilby wasn't impressed. "Maybe we can make it up here today; maybe we slip and go 500 feet on to those rocks. But I'm not going to try and come up here over-balanced with a heavy pack tomorrow and then come down later again with antlers on too. The hell with it. Let's get down off this cliff while we're in one piece!"

Wilby is a pretty good mate, amenable usually to my choice of routes, but perhaps he had a point.

While we chewed a slice or two of steak, two or three keas came swooping down, calling raucously and joyfully to their mates. Tame and very curious, they hopped gradually closer. Wilby was focussing on one kea which was testing his .303 barrel with a strong beak, when another inquisitive bird landed on his shoulder. I've never seen so many keas; I counted twenty-three perched all around.

A mile or two back down the valley Wilby's stag was no longer visible or roaring, though hinds were still scattered

Stalker Russell Sattrup looks across to Mt Aspiring, the peak on the right. Below lies the East Branch of the Matukituki.

High up on the saddle between Mill Creek and East Branch of Matukituki lies a handsome trophy. The stag's harem of thirteen hinds ploughed the snow trail over the tops to the Albert Saddle.

Above: Doug Johnston stows his gear aboard Jimmie Ballantyne's dinghy. A moment later a ten-foot swell surged over the rock Doug stands on.

The Fearful Crags and Canyons of Fiordland. Author with the great sixteen-pointer, high above the canyon of the Light River.

placidly all across the cold southern sub-alpine scrub slope.

"There is nothing here in the headwaters. I'm going after that stag," announced Wilby.

"Okay. I'll go down the valley floor. Might be able to see him and wave you on to him."

Wilby disappeared up through the boulders and scrub, soon becoming a tiny dark moving dot, hardly visible. The sharp-eyed hinds soon spotted me, though, while I was still over half a mile below. When they relaxed a little I crept closer, from boulder to giant boulder, but soon two or three different hinds were staring all too intently my way. Crouching under a huge boulder I spotted the stag, now low on the slope, lying on an outcropping white rock. I was only some five or six hundred yards away, but Wilby was still climbing steadily, now far above under the cliffs and up among the scattered hinds. Once or twice he paused and glanced back for me and I waved my bright red down jacket frantically from beneath the rock, but he never saw me. We were a mile apart and Wilby was expecting me way downstream.

As a hunting experience it was one of my most exciting interludes with a full view of the whole drama. Cautiously Wilby stepped on to a snowgrass rise. A hind threw up her head, stared, pranced away, gathering a little band of other deer. Way down the mountain two more hinds sneaked into cover. Wilby stepped across, the deer moving uneasily. Soon there would be general panic, the whole mob in flight. The stag stood up, looking suspiciously up toward his herd. Now Wilby saw him, threw himself down across a white stone to aim. The range was long—400 yards downhill, maybe further. I saw the great stag flinch and stagger before the distant gunshot reached me. The stag stood miserably hunched but when Wilby stood up after a moment or two I realised my mate could no longer sight his target, hidden in scrub.

I scooped up my 30.06, levered a shell into the breech, flung myself across a jagged rock. Range and bullet drop? Five hundred yards or further? I aimed three feet over the stag's shoulder, squeezed the trigger and hit the target. The stag disappeared into a belt of dense scrub jungle, while both Wilby and I hurried in from widely different angles. A close finishing shot and Wilby had his trophy, a very pretty fourteen-pointer. As we had figured with the glasses, the bay tines were poor, one missing altogether, the other very short. But the tops, crowned with four long tines on the left antler, five on the right, were magnificent. We were delighted. It's not often you pass up a fourteen at daybreak, come back that evening and shoot him.

On 3 April we were away early, climbing straight up the southern wall of the canyon for the tops. Late the previous night the binoculars had sighted a little herd of deer, six hinds and a promising stag, huddled on a narrow snowgrass ledge up along the cliffs. It was a lovely morning, fog in the valley below, ragged peaks thrusting above the clouds. We climbed a little staircase watercourse up to the walls, then struggled hand over hand up a vertical wall clothed in dense virgin scrub. There was little danger of falling, but it was a nightmare struggle, fighting, heaving, hauling up, straight up, into the tangled bushes.

The open rock and snowgrass slope above was steep, sparse of vegetation on a granite base. We climbed carefully, aware that any slip was going to let us roll and fall 1,000 feet. I wouldn't call it dangerous, just very steep and unpleasant. Deer sign was negligible—there was nothing much to eat there—and we followed out a faint trail on to a snowgrass ledge, and scrambled thankfully toward the saddle high above.

Lily Valley isn't very wide; the canyon was barely a mile or so wide in the valley, and not much broader at the top 4,000 feet above. Way across on the cliffs beyond camp, a lone stag poised above a fearful bluff, roaring vociferously. He was safe—we weren't going after him or a little herd of deer I sighted on the high knob between Lily Creek and Iceberg Lake.

Zigzagging up the rocky snowgrass ledges we surprised two little bands of red deer near the crest. They eyed us a moment or two, then went dashing along under the bluffs before climbing for the divide.

"We had better get over the top before those deer disturb the other side," I exclaimed.

We hurried the last few yards, then recoiled in dismay. A tremendous precipice dropped sheer, 2,000 feet, into a cold, blue lake ringed by snow-capped peaks.

The scenery was superb, gigantic cliffs, winding canyons, dazzling mountains. To the east the canyon below wound away to join the Neale Burn; north-west we could see the headwaters of the North Clinton and further round, the sheer mountains which ring Joe's River and the Cleddau beyond.

We climbed to a rise and were having a bit to eat when I spotted a huge black stag, way along on a ledge, probably two miles away. I could barely sight him with the binoculars. I suggested perhaps the stag had come down a ledge off our range, but Wilby was adamant.

"Nothing can get down that cliff. More likely he has tried to get up and can't."

It's amazing how sound carries. I clapped my hands and bellowed, and through the glasses we saw the stag raise his head and look our way. We watched awhile, then roared again, and though the stag didn't answer he finally started picking his way slowly towards us along a deer trail on the steep, sunny ledge. We snatched up our things, slid off the skyline and headed to meet him in the saddle. Even that wasn't straightforward. Two or three times we were stopped by small bluffs and had to backtrack. On one steep pinch I found some intriguing rock samples. Golden mica, or fools' gold, is quite common thereabouts, but this was an odd formation of dull silver discs, projecting an inch or two from the tough white rocks. The unusual mineral looked like the torn pages from a battered book and has since been identified as sheet mica. With the butt of my knife and a sharp rock I hammered off a few samples, stuffed them into a plastic bag and hurried off to stalk our black stag.

By now the stag had moved a mile or more along the ledge, and was directly below the saddle, six feet out from us and 350 yards straight below. The canyon walls still stretched unbroken, untamed for miles each way.

The stag was magnificent—sleek, dull red hide glittering in the sun. The antlers were outstanding, carrying at least a dozen great long points. We estimated the length of beam at something around forty-two inches long, spread probably about thirty-six, with bay tines a little weak, no more than six inches. Top points were exciting, around a foot in length. A dream trophy.

"Do we shoot him?"

Two fairly important considerations checked us. Though only six feet out from our divide he was in the Neale Burn block, and we don't shoot up the other chap's block. Our Fiordland Park permit covered the North Clinton and Joe's River area.

Wilby was quite determined.

"Don't shoot him, Keith. I know you. You'll break your bloody neck before you leave that head lying down there."

I would too.

"We have sixty feet of nylon," I countered. "I can get down those rocks on to that bit of snowgrass."

"Then where?"

He was right. There was still a three or four hundred foot straight drop.

"I still feel there may be a sloping narrow ledge where we first saw the stag," I suggested.

One thing we surely didn't want and that was to kill such an outstanding trophy and then be forced to leave him to rot on the mountain. Far better to leave him to breed or for another lucky stalker.

The stag wasn't roaring, only once did he lift his head and give a half-hearted answer when I bellowed. Savagely he attacked a sturdy silver-leaved mountain bush, then strolled unseeing past three disappointed red hinds. Sadly indecisive, we watched the mountain monarch walk down to a little mountain lake far below, and step casually into the cool water and swim to a rocky point. The stag stepped ashore but, instead of following the short grass of the shoreline again, swam a narrow inlet, then waded deep along the beach.

The stag horned another bush, polishing his antlers, then suddenly trotted purposefully down the canyon toward the Neale Burn.

Did we do the right thing? We will never know, but I hope some young fellow hangs that stag on the wall and I'd like to hear the story when he does.

We climbed miles high along the divide to the south, but feed is sparse on those high rocky tops. Wilby and I saw one group of deer, but didn't disturb them. We both had two cameras each. The day was glorious, so we shot off quite a few photos before descending the canyon wall to camp.

Next morning Wilby headed upstream to stalk a stag roaring in the upper birches, while I stalked down the valley. A stiff frost made the snowgrass wet and cold. Two or three deer were roaring in the bush back in an area of rough moraine and tangled granite. I went in and stalked close to a beast in very dense cover. He roared across a shingle fan. Late the night before I had stalked close to a stag bellowing in the ribbonwood; I could see his body clearly but not the antlers, so didn't shoot. The wind had changed suddenly, the stag had bolted, and so I had lost a possible trophy.

I couldn't see the antlers on this stag either, but when he roared and stepped between the trees I fired. I was somewhat disgusted to find it was a nine-pointer of poor quality, probably better culled out.

Wilby's stag bolted from the bush, raced down across the creek and climbed high up the trail which the wapiti had used to escape the first evening. Range was long but my mate is a very fine shot.

"Just as well we tested our rifles thoroughly before we left home," Wilby said. "This rifle is sighted in just a bit low on your 350-yard range and I was hitting him low too. First time I've nearly emptied the magazine for years, I guess."

His was a nine-pointer too.

Our goal had been Joe's River and still was, but access from the Clinton wasn't easy. We had already hunted Lily Creek fairly thoroughly—the area wasn't large—and the main valley of the North Clinton was supposed to have another party of four hunters in by now.

"What say we go back down to Glade House, boat to Te Anau and drive round to Milford and try the Joe from that side," I suggested. Wilby agreed.

We reached the cullers' old tent camp late that evening and while Wilby wet his fly line for a trout, I splashed across the now shallow Clinton. Boots splish-splashing, full of water, aren't very suitable to stalk in and I had hardly stepped ashore when a stag roared belligerently clear and loud from the birches right ahead. I eased a shell into the breech, hastily dragged off my hobnail boots and emptied a pint of river water from each and lashed them on again. Bare feet are no good on those coarse sharp rocks.

A recent landslide had spewed a fan of gravel through the birches, burying some trees and covering all the undergrowth. I soon saw the stag, a little six-pointer striding across the opening. I let him go, then swung around as more hooves clattered on the gravel. A startled and badly frightened ten-pointer hastened by. Wilby had been fishing just downstream when he had spooked the deer.

Next day we tramped back down the Clinton. Roaring was negligible in the valley apart from one occasion, when a distant stag roared high on the steep bush cliffs. Another stag roared violently from close by. Off came the packs, rifles were checked, and we walked quietly up through the trees.

We came on him suddenly, standing poised by a large birch. A glimpse of tall commanding antlers brought the rifle sweeping up. The stag crashed away at the gunshot and collapsed in a depression lovely with the graceful Prince of Wales Feather ferns. A fine big stag, and a good length of antler, but only nine points again.

Wilby tried his hand at the rainbows near the Forks but had no luck. We met three fishermen-hunters near there too, in for a weekend of casual stalking or fishing.

We unloaded our rifles by the Milford Track and spent some time stalking a lone blue mountain duck with the cameras. Hiking down the track, a tractor and trailer came careering down, piloted by a cheerful bearded young character known as Darky.

"What are you, Track Ranger or Track Deerstalker?" I enquired, indicating the load of three or four stags, plus men and rifles aboard the trailer.

Darky grinned. "I'm just the trackman around here, but I'm carting out a carcass or two for Charlie and his mate.

"That's a nice fourteen you have there. Climb aboard," invited Darky.

At Glade House we learnt the *Tarewa* had been delayed picking up a couple of wapiti hunters. Mr and Mrs Dawson, who manage the place for the Tourist Department, hospitably invited us in, fed us coffee and later a very ample dinner.

Somewhere in the bush beyond the swingbridge a stag moaned mournfully.

"That's my fourteen," claimed Darky. "Let him go in the velvet and I'll go after him in a day or two when he's roaring right."

A couple of months previously the 'copters had spent three days hunting the tops and headwaters of the Neale and North Clinton, and had taken out 312 carcasses, almost all hinds. Perhaps this was why deer had seemed rather scarce on the high tops.

The *Tarewa* didn't reach Te Anau until near midnight. Wilby and I bedded down in Stuart's bach, and headed down to the Deerstalkers' Wapiti Lodge early next day for a quick shower and clean-up. Two resident Te Awamutu stalkers, Hubble Hall and Red Pratt, hospitably gave us breakfast which saved unpacking, then we were off on the road to Milford.

It's a lovely drive but we wasted no time, reaching Milford Sound around lunchtime. We hoped to arrange some transport across Milford Sound that afternoon.

The Assistant Manager of the Milford Hotel turned out to be a cousin I had never met before. He was very helpful and so was Mick Arthur when I approached him in the Far West Bar later on. Known as the Lake Ada Pirate, Mick pilots a jetboat up and down Lake Ada with supplies for Quintin Hut. Uniform in the Far West Bar seems to be hobnail boots and parka, for it is the hangout of the crayfishermen, deerstalkers and trackmen.

"I know you," said Mick. "You're Keith Severinsen and I saw your Alaska slides at Taupo. How's Jack Dillon?"

"Haven't seen Jack, but he's wapiti hunting in the Lower Glaisnock right now." You can't get far in New Zealand without all your stalking acquaintances keeping track of your hunting fortunes.

We crossed Freshwater Bay at 8 am next morning in a Tourist Department launch, along with a load of diesel oil and paper cups for Quintin Hut. There were also two Australian girls aboard, waitresses from Milford Hotel, and Ray the packhorse man. At Sandfly Point the trailer was loaded, then a battered Faircrough tractor bumped us three miles up the Track toward Lake Ada. The seat was long gone and at least one bag of chaff had never reached Ray's packhorses. It was used as a substitute seat on the old tractor, bright green sprouts shooting profusely from the rotting bag.

Mick roared off up Lake Ada in his jetboat, taking the girls, Ray, and supplies on the first load.

"Be back for you in half an hour. Bring down that fourteen-foot aluminium dinghy from Doughboy and I'll lend it to you to get up the Joe. Too many snags for the jet. Ripped a hole in her last week."

We balanced the dinghy atop the jet craft and crouched beneath to cruise the three miles of Lake Ada. Considerable care is needed in navigating the lake, as it was formed long ago by a giant landslide, and the drowned trees still snag unwary boats.

The mouth of Joe's River is deep, slow, and dark, winding into a broad estuary before snaking back into the Joe River canyon. Mick off loaded us and roared off in his jet.

Wilby didn't trust me with the oars so I navigated, directing him between the tree snags and shallows. There were brown trout everywhere, beautiful fish, swimming lazily ahead of the dinghy. Once there was a flotilla of five fish swimming abreast and later Wilby said quietly, "Look, Keith!" Right under the oar a huge deep-bodied fish eyed him balefully. It must have weighed ten pounds.

On a narrow sandspit I leapt ashore, loaded with my own cameras and Wilby's movie. The scenery everywhere was superb, but what took my eye on the sand was the hoof marks of a huge deer with a print like a wapiti. The stream narrowed to a fairly shallow ripple so I waded ahead pulling the boat on a rope.

There was a deep pool ahead which required considerable manoeuvring between the snags. I glanced upstream to see a stag leaping into the toe-toe. Another fine stag was following. I roared, and the second stag stopped, looking our way. The number of points I couldn't count, but a fine spread swept up to flaring tops. I snatched up the rifle and tried to draw a bead standing in the gently rocking boat. Range was 150 yards and the scope sight danced wildly back and forth.

"You can't hit him, Keith. Wait until I get you ashore."

The stag watched a moment until we were almost in the shallows, then darted after his mate. We dragged the boat high above the stream, secured it carefully and tied the rowlocks and oars high in a tree. That's flood country around Milford!

We were surprised to find it was already 1 pm, so we hitched on our packs and headed up the Joe. Rainforest growth was prolific and there didn't appear ever to have been a deer nibbling this lush vegetation. With the absence of deer browsing signs, an odd fact was a well-defined deer trail winding upstream. Luxuriant ferns actually met over our heads and many species of them are relished by deer.

Wilby and I, fairly fit by now, tramped the first one and a half hours without pause until the rapids eased off and a small, scrubby clearing was reached. We had seen only one deer, a small six-point stag, and had heard only one roar.

A few years previously there had been a huge landslide further upstream, just below the Talbot confluence. The landslide had swept the canyon wall clear of vegetation and trees for a whole half-mile, crushing out a broad, scarred clearing at the base. Joe's River was quite wide and shallow hereabouts, and when we sighted deer in shade near the far bank we crossed to stalk closer. But they were only another six-point stag and a lone hind.

We were tramping up the boulder stream when there was a sudden close roar from the trees to our right. I ditched my pack and glanced about for Wilby. He had his pack off too and, rifle in hand, was crouching alert, rifle covering the wide river. Wondering if the stag was already eyeing me from the trees, I hurried across the gravel.

There was a steep ten-foot bank to negotiate, slick and still damp from the last flood. I stepped hastily on to a smooth five-finger sapling and my boot shot away with a horrible clatter. I swung up the rifle toward the bank above, expecting an angry stag's head to investigate the noise. Nothing. Quickly I climbed the knotted roots to a more advantageous position and peered into the trees.

An enormous stag stood only ten yards away, head hidden behind a large birch. White-tipped antlers, three to a crown, waved backwards. I didn't hesitate further but fired.

It was a very disappointing royal. Antler-length topped about thirty-seven and a half inches, and spread thirty-one and a half inches, but the points were all rather short. One bay was weak and the other broken off. The stag was tremendous, the biggest red deer I had ever seen. We removed the antlers to photograph them in the open streambed, then left them there for the next flood. One back steak weighed twelve or fifteen pounds, and kept us in excellent meat for several days.

Searching for a reasonable campsite we pushed on, following the deer trail up through heavy bush alongside a rumbling rapid. Near Surprise Creek the Joe smoothed out and here was a lovely place to camp, on a sandy dry opening of perhaps half an acre. There was no sign that deer had ever trimmed the abundant grass, or men stalked the valley.

Walking from the island at the mouth of Joe's River to Surprise Creek junction took us until only 5.30 pm. Included in that period was a meal, stalking a couple of stags, and fooling around photographing one of them, the twelve-pointer. It's excellent travelling up the Joe.

Near our camp two blue mountain ducks preened themselves and we heard the peculiar drumming of a weka.

Rain clouds were piling up on the morning of 8 April. We had an early breakfast and were on the trail at daylight which wasn't until 7.20 in that deep canyon. Travelling was still good, either on a well-defined deer trail on either bank, or along the various boulder beaches. Higher up the Joe, where the valley narrowed, we noted that the deer trail took care to cross at the best fords and avoided the moraine debris. Apart from the deer trail, there was no sign of any animals. We heard no roars and the only fresh tracks were the marks of one huge stag which led steadily downriver all the way. Perhaps it was the stag I had already shot. Rubmarked trees, mostly pepperwoods, so fresh they still oozed sap, were quite plentiful, and all the marks were impressive. Several we measured at seven feet six inches above the ground. One old, cast antler, moss-covered, was picked up but wasn't exciting. It was a short antler with six poor points.

Joe's River climbs easily, with no great gorges or waterfalls, and toward noon the trail led into a shingle reach. The canyon swings south again here, and we had a view of the Marshall Pass a mile or so high ahead. We had tramped steadily for three hours without pause, so stayed for a quick snack in the bush. Another half-hour's tramp led us out to the moraine scrub below the pass, three and a half hours' actual travelling time, without a pack, from our Surprise Creek camp.

I roared a few times but no deer answered, which wasn't surprising considering the almost entire lack of fresh sign. I don't think there was one deer in the whole valley above our camp. Rain and mist were settling in steadily, which rather dampened any thought of climbing the Marshall Pass and looking down to Iceberg Lake and the Clinton.

At the shingle reach a mile below the pass, a few deer had lingered and trimmed the vegetation. We wondered if several big stags had secreted in there during the velvet, rubbed up their antlers and moved out of the Joe for the roar. It was noticeable that the fuchsias were most favoured, with five-fingers second; the latter already had fresh replacement leaves an inch long.

Near camp we were rather startled to note fresh bootmarks.

That was odd in an area as remote and mountain-girt as the Joe Canyon. The last of the Morioris don't wear hobnails. About 4 pm we crossed the Joe to hunt up Surprise Creek before rain and flooded rivers halted further exploring. One hundred and fifty yards into the moss-encrusted bush a stag roared.

"We won't roar an answer," I whispered. "Could be the other stalker." Warily we closed in.

The stag roared again, well to the right.

"It's a stag all right, and he's travelling. I'll stay here and roar him—hold his attention, while you go after him."

While I gave an occasional bellow Wilby stalked ahead. Moss, deep and soft, shrouded every twig and boulder, making quiet movement easy. Steady rain damped our scent. I heard the stag give a startled alarm cough and Wilby's roar as he tried to halt the stag's flight. My mate came back, explaining that the stag had been sneaking quietly in towards me, and Wilby and the stag had surprised each other. It may have been a ten-pointer, Wilby considered, but certainly not a spectacular trophy lost.

We wandered into an oozing Tanekaha swamp, deep in moss and bog, and fought our way through to Surprise Creek. It ran in a narrow defile which we crossed. The forest beyond was swampy and uninviting, so we gradually circled back towards camp. Rather surprisingly, we had been gone an hour and a half.

It rained steadily through the night, and by morning the river was rising rapidly. I marked the stream and it rose six inches during breakfast. Thunder rumbled up the Joe and rain teemed down. We waited for a while before deciding to abandon the upper Joe and head downstream. After all, we obviously couldn't cross the Joe for some days, and there was no roaring or indication of deer on our narrow bench beneath the canyon walls.

Preparing for a wet and miserable journey we packed the base of our packs with the billies, meat, tins of butane gas—anything that water in the bottom of the pack couldn't hurt. Spare clothes, cameras, and sleeping bags went into their plastic containers in the driest part, that is the middle of the pack. We wrung out our wet trousers from the previous day, quickly donned them, then when everything loose in the tent was packed, collapsed the tent and fly and strapped them atop the load. I hate removing a scope sight from a rifle but the Meopta 4 X had been fogging a little, and a day's soaking might ruin it. I shoved it down the pack too.

Away down the Joe deer trail, the river a surging, raging, rampant giant on our right. Twice we passed under huge logs lying astride the track. Previously deer had sheltered from storm under them; vegetation was tramped and muddied, but strangely no deer had sheltered there during the present tempest. My twelve-point deer still sat propped forlornly in the riverbed, now surrounded by rising flood waters. Oddly enough it had been swung about since we saw it last, and balanced carefully anew by some human hand.

We couldn't cross the river now to stalk the clearing; in fact we saw nothing all day to indicate a deer left in the Joe, for we walked from Surprise Creek to Lake Ada and not one deer had even crossed the trail. We lunched briefly on crumbled, damp sandwiches, steak and biscuits, watching a lone shag wing up the flooded torrent, disappearing in the rain clouds.

It was 3.45 pm when we gladly dumped our packs by the dinghy and set about putting up camp in the sodden, dripping rainforest. The tea billy went on the primus while we cut poles and pegs, strung up the tent and fly. Bundles of black, damp fern were spread deep on the floor of the tent, then a plastic sheet atop the wet fern made a springy mattress. Wilby, in spite of woollen "waterproof" smock and oilskin parka, was saturated to the hide and shivering, but my new heavy nylon parka had kept me dry. Wilby crawled into his sleeping bag to thaw out but I headed downstream towards Lake Ada with the rifle and came to a deep, amber backwater flooded dark and deep. Way back in the pepperwoods and birches, a worn deer trail led gamely into the still menacing water. I studied the crossing without enthusiasm. Snow tipped the tussock tops—there wasn't a fresh deer trail anywhere since dawn, nor a solitary roar to brighten a drear evening. It rained softly, steadily. One thing alone made me step reluctantly waist-deep into the chill, dark pool. It was a pepperwood standing naked, stripped clean of bark eight feet above the ground. It was a mighty stag that had done that!

I crawled dripping from the pool, water squelching from my trousers and each boot, but there was no stag ahead that night. I stalked the moss-hung jungle to Lake Ada, and circled way back up the Joe and out to a shingle bar above camp. At last one stag answered my challenge, roaring deep and angry from the tall bush across river above the estuary island. I crouched in the toe-

toe, trying to roar him out to cross the river, but I heard him roar again faintly twice as he departed northwards toward Milford.

Snow crested the range next morning. The rain had temporarily departed, but a roaring, blustery gale swirled down the Joe and came sweeping down the Arthur. There were fresh deer tracks, big ones too, churning my own prints of the previous evening.

With the swirling gale, chances of a successful bush stalk were nil, but I said to Wilby: "I can see new deer sign on the island. They seem to like it there and this appears to be their only shallow ford. What say one of us wades the Joe, goes downstream and comes back up through the bush on the island. If they are hiding there, they may break across the ford here, like the other day."

"Funny thing, but I was wondering the same thing. Anyway, it's worth a try."

Wilby settled behind a stump while I waded the smaller branch of the Joe. The river had dropped four feet overnight and the crossing was now only knee-deep. But there were no deer on the island, only fresh tracks of their passing. Just another long chance which didn't pay off!

Snow, rain, seething gales gave no chance of further successful stalking so we broke camp, bailed the dinghy dry and headed downstream. Wilby still didn't trust me handling the oars, so I used a long lancewood sapling to fend off snags or shallows. A strong current hurled us downstream, then a terrific gust of wind would send the dinghy spinning out of control. Once or twice we climbed overboard to rope the dinghy down between snags and rapids. Downstream Lake Ada and the Joe River estuary were three feet deeper with the flood. That's right, a lake three miles long had risen three feet overnight. Instead of snaking through the sandbars, deep holes, and shallows of the estuary, there was an angry lake four to five hundred yards across, with a terrific gale sweeping down the Arthur River driving piled white-capped waves ahead. We didn't know it at the time, but right then a cyclone was devastating Wellington and Christchurch, driving the *Wahine* to disaster on Barrett's Reef.

Wilby heaved on the oars, but the storm still swept us toward the flooded trees. I poled desperately in the shallower patches, yelling instructions which oar to pull on to straighten our weaving, erratic course. Halfway across the estuary wind and waves swept us headlong toward the trees, so I grabbed a drowning manuka bush and hung on grimly. We were close to shipwreck that moment. Then came a lull in the storm. Wilby heaved on the oars again and we were into deeper, sheltered water down the Joe, with Lake Ada ahead. The sandbar of Lake Ada was completely exposed to the gale, so we both went overboard, managing to drag and rope the dinghy up into the Arthur River between gusts.

Earlier we had heard the Lake Ada Pirate go past in his jet-boat, but whether up or down we didn't know. While Wilby waited with the boat I hurried up the Milford Track, eager to catch Mick at the boatsheds if possible. Making time, I wasn't too intent on the magnificent scenery until passing Steep Mountain just south of Poseidon Creek there came a rumbling, thundering, intermittent roar, like the sound of jet aircraft. It was the mountain trying to fall on top of me. The cyclonic gale was loosening trees and vegetation high on the cliffs, three to four thousand feet above, and once a slip started it snowballed, with thousands of tons of rock, scrub, and whole living trees cascading, tumbling, pouring in a magnificent spectacle down the cliffs. I was 100 yards or so out from the base of the cliffs with considerable bush between, but since I was directly below the mountain I didn't waste too much time standing and watching. Five slips rumbled down while I hurried past.

Mick Arthur was still at the boatshed with several other track employees, watching the landslides hurtling off Steep Mountain.

When I questioned Mick about other hunters in the Joe he was emphatic that no one had gone in across Lake Ada. So how did those bootmarks get there? Maybe someone ventured down Surprise Creek, or a party pioneered the Talbot off the tops toward the Cleddau. Or a helicopter dropped them in?

We picked up Wilby with the jetboat, and headed the craft into the stormy waves of Lake Ada. Our first Joe's River hunt was over.

New country, unknown, intriguing. I'm going back to the Joe, to explore the Talbot to its source, see what lies up the Surprise Creek canyon. Maybe, somewhere up the Joe, lives the mightiest stag in all Fiordland.

West to the Whitewater River

Wapiti Hunting in Fiordland

EVENING SHADOWS were darkening the valley of the Whitewater as the fishing craft *Koromiko* surged down lonely George Sound. I swung my binoculars to scan a narrow strip of yellow snow-grass, bright in the late afternoon sun, poised on a ledge 4,000 sheer feet above the sound.

"Not much ground up there!" I remarked to my mates. "But that little sheltered basin just could hold a bull. It's a bit steep getting there, though."

"Call them 'Horror Peaks'," muttered Russell. They were, too. An unknown, unnamed, jagged series of scarred, battered mountains, each piercing spectacularly skyward, ribbed with water-torn crevasses and slashed by granite chasms, east of the Whitewater River, girt by the south-west arm of George Sound.

It was Sunday 26 March 1967 and we were off to Fiordland into the wapiti country, to hear again the bugle of a bull elk, and watch the morning mists weaving across the sounds.

With two well-tested mates, Wilby Oliver of Hawke's Bay and Russell Sattrup of Waikato, I had left the North Island three or four days before, crossed the straits to Lyttelton by ferry, then driven south next day, reaching Mararoa sheep station just short of Te Anau. Allan Bradley greeted us and forecast there would be no flying start early next morning.

"You could do a shoot along Prospect Mountain at daybreak and be back here by 10 o'clock to ring the aerodrome," he said. "Bernie Chaney will drive you three chaps out with his rover and spread yourselves along the southern bush edge. Pick a good knob each for you never know what the dogs will put up. I'll ride in by Dawson City with the pack and stir up those birch gullies where Keith and Bill Koller helped rope the boar."

Black rain clouds surged across Lake Te Anau to the west as next morning we tramped through the drenched snowgrass to our stands. I was more or less in the middle of the ragged two-mile line of rifles when I heard a single shot miles to the south. That would be Allan somewhere on the high hill above the sagging, mustering shanty christened "Dawson City".

Two black, hurrying forms caught my eye, coming through a

shallow hollow. I swung up the binoculars. Yes, a couple of good pigs all right.

The wild pigs veered right, crossed a swamp somewhat to one side and disappeared in the snowgrass. Leaving my stand I ran to cut them off and reached the edge of a deep, hidden gorge just as the two animals came trotting up the edge. Bang. One pig was down. Another shot, and the second pig sprawled in the snowgrass. Both wild tuskers were quite dead so I turned and hurried the quarter-mile back to my rise. Nothing more came my way. Russell Sattrup was stationed way across the gorge, and once I glimpsed two deer slipping into the bush far beyond him. They must have been flushed from the bush past him, or crept up the gorge between us.

Allan Bradley rode up. He had himself bailed and shot a very large boar earlier, and seen several more deer disappearing.

I was surprised at the size of the two pigs I had bowled. One was a boar, but the other was a sleek, fat barrow.

"That's the same pig we roped and carried home in the rover three years ago!" exclaimed Allan. "Here is that scar on his back, remember . . . and the Mararoa earmark I snicked in his ear."

It's a long chance to return three years later and kill the same animal; it was the identical pig all right. Jack, Allan's strong saddle horse, was well used to packing game, but didn't altogether approve of two wild pigs on him. We finished trudging down Prospect Creek in the rain, Russell balancing one pig, myself the other, taking all the weight we could alongside old Jack.

Put on the scales outside the game freezer unit at the homestead, Allan's boar scaled 180 pounds dressed, mine 160, and the barrow 190.

By the way, in the last year Allan Bradley and Bernie Chaney had put 466 deer in that freezer, all taken from Mararoa. There are still a few deer in Southland, but the Government cullers said that they had to be drastically reduced on Mararoa or they would step in.

Early on Saturday morning we packed and headed into Te Anau, ready for a quick airlift if the weather allowed. While we waited, car after car of exuberant wapiti hunters rolled into the township. Many of the chaps I knew. Most parties would go across the lake into the eastern wapiti blocks next morning per

This whitetail buck was a fine old animal, but the horns are past their prime.

Wilby Oliver takes his trophy for a ride in the tractor tube dinghy, George Sound.

Wilby Oliver with his Saddle Hill trophy.

A dead kiwi found high on the snowgrass ridge above George Sound.

WEST TO THE WHITEWATER RIVER

the *Tarewa*, but the majority of stalkers wished to arrange a prior airdrop of supplies.

No aircraft flew that day. The float plane dipped and wallowed at her moorings and the Grumman amphibian wasn't in sight. Rain and snow swept across the peaks of Fiordland.

When the Milford telephone line opened late on Saturday morning, I put a call through and managed at last to contact a fishing man willing to take us down. A boat trip from Milford to George Sound had been our hope all along. Flying is fun, but Fiordland weather and its inevitable delays can be frustrating.

Cancelling our flight plan, we headed the rover for Milford Sound, and by late next day were cruising up George Sound. The *Koromiko* had left Milford at 9 am with three parties of hunters aboard. Allan Harrison and his three mates, Alistair McDonald, John Banford, and Peter Benlove had the George River block, so we dropped them ashore away up Bligh Sound. Late in the afternoon we put another three hunters ashore, Lloyd Wills of Wellington and his party. They were rowed to the sandy beach of the George River by Skull, a cheerful Maori fisherman.

The 1967 wapiti trophy period was arranged differently from previous seasons. For quite a few years now, the wapiti territory of Fiordland—almost all that ragged array of tangled mountains and fiords west from Lake Te Anau to the sea—had been divided into twenty-odd stalking blocks with a three- or four-man party allocated to each area by ballot. But many of the hunting blocks are so large or precipitous that one party just couldn't stalk its area efficiently in two or three weeks, and some didn't try.

For years the New Zealand Deerstalkers' Association has arranged and partly financed scores of deer culling trips into the wapiti territory to thin down undesirable wapiti and shoot back the encroaching red deer. In 1967 the Fiordland National Park Board took control and demanded a drastic reduction in the wapiti and red deer herds with a policy of arranging widescale shooting parties. If you wished to stalk for a trophy bull wapiti, you either qualified by acting as a culler, or put up the cash to pay for culling operations. The amount was substantial, $60 for a South Islander and $40 for the more distant North Islanders. Instead of only one party per block, three parties could all stalk one particular area.

This was one of the main reasons we applied for the remote sprawling Whitewater block—plenty of elbow room to hunt without wondering where the next stalking party would be. Bruce Smith and Joe Leslie, two Australian boys, were landing by George Barnby's crayfish boat in isolated Looking Glass Bay, twenty miles west of us. S. Larsen from Lumsden and his mate were flying in by amphibian plane to the mouth of the Whitewater River. They intended to hunt the inviting snowgrass tops sprawling west of the Whitewater toward the Tasman.

Russell Sattrup, Wilby Oliver and I were landing at the head of the south-west arm of George Sound, at the mouth of the Ethne Stream. So far as we could ascertain every Whitewater party for many years had landed in the Whitewater River area itself and had completely neglected the isolated and jagged region east and west of the Ethne Saddle. We hoped so anyway, as towards dark the *Koromiko* chugged up the sound. The water was deep and dark, so deep that the fifty-foot fishing boat just nosed straight up the beach and we went ashore over the bow. Rifles, packs, tents, food, fishing gear—within minutes our gear was piled on the stones.

Long ago someone had camped before us at the mouth of rippling Ethne Stream. If we had arrived by aircraft we had intended to use a spartan fly and pup tent as a supply base, but a definite advantage of arriving by sea was being able to take a few extra supplies and a decent-sized 8 x 12 tent. Costs, by the way, between air and sea are more or less comparable. By amphibian into George Sound with a 750-800 pound payload all up (which isn't much) costs about $56 each flight. Float plane is rather less in price but apparently a bit more chancy as the water needs to be fairly smooth, otherwise the float plane flicks on her back. Our sea trip was $100 per party, down and back to Milford.

As the *Koromiko* disappeared into the twilight a stag roared a challenge from the bush above. It was wonderful, ashore at last with the high hills and a fortnight's hunting ahead.

Supplies, films, gear were sorted and we yarned deep into the night. We were on the trail early on Monday morning, however, with a seven-day pack each on our backs. Twenty years ago, in 1947 or 1948, the New Zealand-American Fiordland Expedition had blazed a trail up the Ethne Stream and down toward their main base in the Stillwater. A few axe marks still showed, but we lost time every occasion we traversed the Ethne trail trying without much success to follow the old track. Not that it mattered, for in the valley the moss-covered bush was open and pleasant, though deer sign was negligible. A mile up the Ethne Stream there was a small clearing where long ago shingle had spilled and buried the bush. Dense young beeches, struggling for the sun, had almost choked the opening, but the few deer in the watershed all lived nearby. They too sought the sun and light.

We saw our first wapiti from the clearing when I swung my glass back across the sound, high up to the crest of Horror Peaks. On a steeply-sloping southern face, sandwiched between a precipice and a rocky spine, grazed four or five golden wapiti, bright in the morning sun. Judging by size, one was a bull, but they were at least two, maybe three miles away.

Russell would have turned straight back, struggled a couple of miles around the shore of the sound and slogged upwards, but Wilby and I vetoed that idea. Perhaps Wilby and I were wrong —who knows—but we had ideas of circling back to Horror Peaks and the herd from away to the west. The three of us climbed steadily to Ethne Saddle, swung west and up steeply toward the tops. The forest was heavy beech, with prolific fern and plant growth showing no sign of deer. In the base of one dry hollow tree we found the nest of a large bird, probably a kiwi or weka.

The slope steadily became steeper until we pulled up short, with a sheer cliff rearing ahead. Knowing there should be an old deer trail somewhere, I poked about to the left, but without success. Russell had crawled some way up the cliff and climbed down again to report a reasonable route. He and Wilby measure around five feet ten, I'd estimate, but I'm only a little bloke. Russell and Wilby led the way up the cliff, scaling from tree to tree, but soon I found myself dangling over sixty feet of nothingness, stretching vainly for a branch that I just couldn't reach.

"Hey!" I called. "You fellows will have to pull me up. I'm just not long enough to make it."

Wilby precariously unhitched his pack, handed it to Russell to balance while he returned, wedged himself against a root and reached his rifle down for me to swing up on.

From then on I led the way, knowing if I could reach a root or branch overhead the others could follow. It was an awful climb, struggling up an absolutely perpendicular cliff for the next two or three hours. Where scar or slip left the granite without any vegetation whatever we edged precariously right or left along a narrow ledge, but mostly we climbed straight up, from root to tree, sometimes climbing the shaking tree trunks themselves and then scrambling from the upper branches on to the ledge above. The heavy sixty-pound packs had to be forced and smashed ever upwards through the dense virgin vegetation. Rifles tangled on our shoulders, put us off-balance as we hauled upwards, clutching madly for the next handhold, feet kicking desperately for a toe grip in the loose moss and swaying branches. A dozen times one plunging rifle or another was nearly lost, for we had to thrust the weapons into the limbs or roots overhead, then struggle upwards through the scrub without dislodging them.

A thousand feet above I sprawled suddenly over the rim, up at last on the high divide. The ridge was like a knife-edge with the sombre trees a thousand or fifteen hundred feet below, back where we had just come from. The weather was glorious, the sky blue and cloudless. Wilby and I traced the course of the Stillwater, recalling old campsites and crossings of our last trip there fifteen years before.

Packs on again, up along the crest of the ridge, through stunted birch and celery pine we tramped steadily, eager to be out on the tops to camp the night. The spur was ribbed by nasty chasms, screened in the trees, but an old deer trail, long unused, wound down, along and up out of each obstacle. But late in the evening we had a real setback when we found that the whole range split apart and dropped 1,000 feet down into a hidden basin with an entrancing dark lake cradled in the hollow.

Welcome Lake, as the pool is named on an old forgotten map, is beautiful, the still, shadowed waters reflecting every facet of Virgil Peaks, rearing beyond the Stillwater. In the swamp bush surrounding the lake we angled left to avoid a heavy bluff. We struck a fair wapiti trail and climbed high out on to a rocky spur, then slogged up through the stunted trees toward the peaks again. The spur shelved abruptly and we could see snowgrass 200 yards ahead.

"Drop your pack," I said to Russell. "We'll camp here on this dry knob. Go ahead and see if you can see a bull."

Wilby and I soon had Russell's handy 7 x 7 tent strung up, and since the night was fine, didn't bother with the fly. From our perch on the divide we could gaze straight down into the Stillwater so far below, and toward sunset one wapiti after another appeared to graze the scattered clearings in the middle Stillwater. There must be fifteen acres in the main swampy glade, and by dark fifteen wapiti, coats creamy yellow, grazed the short, sweet grass. One or two were bulls. Through the glasses we watched them stretch out their heads to bugle, but the sound we could scarcely hear. One bull rolled and wallowed in the mud.

Wilby's new gas primus seemed a dead loss; the flame was weak and worthless, so finally in disgust we scouted around and found enough dry leatherwood to cook up rice and a brew of those handy freeze-dried peas mixed with potato powder.

Russell arrived back toward dark, appalled at yet another awful chasm ahead, splitting the ridge asunder, four or five hundred feet deep.

"Couldn't see a track anywhere," he said. "Might get down if the ropes are long enough, but it's a real hellhole." It was a sombre note to end a tough day on the trail, ten hours with the packs on.

Yet another glorious dawn began as we packed camp at daybreak and climbed up over the mountain to inspect the chasm. On the far side the mountain climbed steeply in a pleasant snowgrass slope, but to the north the bush fell almost sheer to the sound, 3,000 and more feet below. On the snowgrass hill a young red stag appeared against the sky on the crest. Then a wapiti bugled loud and clear somewhere in the bush edge between the stag and ourselves. The stag glanced abruptly to look for the wapiti but took no further notice as the bull bugled four or five times again.

I was inclined to think the bull was in heavy birches just across the chasm, but Russ and Wilby believed him to be four or five hundred yards away high in the alpine scrub. A bugle has a deceptively high, ventriloquist note and they're hard to pinpoint. We watched and waited eagerly, hoping the bull would appear on one of the snowgrass ribs fingering into the birches. But the bull didn't move, and knowing the wind was tricky and wouldn't hold, we finally went gingerly to see if we could cross the chasm. An ancient wapiti trail led over the edge, skirted an appalling cliff, wound along a narrow ledge, down a crevasse, back along another ledge, and plunged down a rocky cleft to the bottom. The far wall was steep but not dangerous, with a well-marked deer trail, and soon we were scrambling on to the crest with Russell's rifle in the lead. But the zephyr breeze drifted, a wapiti cow coughed a warning, and that was that!

We camped a couple of miles further on and for the following five days Russell checked the chasm slope. But we neither saw nor heard that bull again. Who said wapiti were dumb, and soon returned to their stamping grounds after being disturbed? Don't you believe it!

From the snowgrass ridge ahead a delightful basin, scattered with tarns, trees and white marble outcrops, sloped away toward Madman's Creek, a forgotten tributary of the Stillwater. Three brown ducks rippled the water of the largest pool. A red stag which lay on a knoll, leapt to his feet, then dashed toward cover. His wapiti cow consort followed a moment then turned and stared curiously our way. For half an hour she watched us before slowly scaling a rock slide on the far slope. Twice a wapiti bugled, once so clearly we believed him on the lake edge just below. Perhaps he was there, but if so we couldn't see him in the scattered trees, tussock and dark koromiko bushes. We didn't like descending too far and disturbing the ground. A few animals bugled far below in Madman's Creek. They were out of our block anyway, so towards noon we climbed back to the divide to stalk our little eight-point red deer.

Russell had his 35 mm Practica (and telephoto lens) loaded with Kodachrome. Wilby had a 35 mm colour slide camera and also a Bell and Howell turret head job 8 mm movie. A very good camera too—I should know because I had just sold it to him!

I was loaded with cameras for a photographic documentary of Fiordland; its mountains and birds, fiords, and wapiti, were my prime objective. Certainly I also wanted a wapiti trophy, but I already had a nice twelve-pointer hanging on the wall, and I wouldn't shoot one smaller. Wilby thought along similar lines, the only difference being that he had a longer, fourteen-pointer, instead of a twelve. I carried a new Asahi Pentax Spotomatic 35 mm camera with telelens, another 35 mm automatic camera loaded with black and white film to use for illustrating stories, and then a Canon 8 mm zoom lens movie camera too. Dangle three cameras, binoculars and a rifle round your neck, and sort that tangle out in a hurry!

The eight-pointer was still sound asleep in the sun, but the click and whirr of six cameras would waken any deer. The red stag jumped up, looked, ran, and climbed on to the skyline before darting down the cliffs. We reached for our map, and spent a pleasant half-hour eating lunch and pinpointing the mountains and valleys disappearing into the tangled peaks of Fiordland.

By a tarn in the snowgrass I found a kiwi. He was a big grey bird, quite heavy, and only dead a few days. The keas had pecked out a handful of feathers, and scattered them around. Wondering what had killed the bird, I dissected it and found the bird apparently healthy, with some body fat and a full stomach. Berries, mainly white-coloured ones, and roots were prominent in the contents. That was the first kiwi alive or dead I'd ever seen in the bush, but they appear to be quite plentiful around George Sound in the snowgrass above the timberline. We saw kiwi footprints in several widely scattered tarns, and fresh beak marks spearing the soil.

By candlelight that evening I skinned the kiwi and eventually it went forward to the Auckland Museum.

We made a pleasant camp on the ridge in a deep saddle where the range was split by yet another wide chasm. There was a glorious view south down the Stillwater watershed to Lake Marchant, north across the George Sound toward Lake Alice and the George River. Late in the evening we spotted the young wapiti bull which had bugled earlier, for from our camp high above we could see down, way down into the park slope 500 or 600 yards below. He was only a light nine-pointer.

Next day was dull and cold with a shivering north-west wind giving notice of rain. Russell had glassed a bull in an inaccessible bush clearing and was convinced he had seen the daddy of all wapiti. Wilby gallantly offered to accompany him so I prospected westwards out on to the high snowgrass tops which straddle the eastern Whitewater watershed.

Once I had fought up through the leatherwood out of the chasm the travelling was excellent, snowgrass with much scattered slab rock of marble origin. A wapiti bugled on the northern cliff face of Expedition Peak, so I stalked him with camera and rifle.

He was a young bull carrying ten even points, length and spread both probably forty-five inches. I reeled off some slides, then stood up to disturb the bull and put some action in the movie. He just watched me, full of interest.

"You're on candid camera," I said, but to no avail. That bull had never seen anything like me before. He was 100 yards below down a bluff, so I left him there, still eyeing me. The sight of man doesn't disturb these unsophisticated animals but man-scent —that's a different matter. Skirting Expedition Peak to the south, I saw three wapiti cows and a spiker on the summit. I passed them quietly but they were still uneasy.

It was a stalker's dream ahead, with a vast snowgrass slope extending three or four miles to the west. Red deer and wapiti were scattered all across it. Bulls were bugling, stags answering with a deep bellowing roar, while other stags imitated the wapiti and bugled. Hurriedly I focussed the glass on one little distant mob.

"No good." Three hinds and a small red stag. A mile away a young wapiti bull, only six or seven points, herded three cows. Somewhere in a hollow close ahead a bull bugled strongly, a high thrilling note, and apparently just beneath me, a red stag answered furiously. I edged cautiously down to see if he was worth stalking, but a small red hind walked aimlessly on to a rise above me, turned and fled. Then the three wapiti cows on the summit came spilling over, frightened, dashing down to join the main herds. Darting into a hollow I ran across it, determined to check the wapiti herd bull before he escaped. Several red deer were filing up from way below and four more wapiti cows were fleeing across a shingle slide.

The bull was poised to follow when I gave a terrific bellow. He swung round, bugling fiercely. A mighty beast but the antlers were not impressive. He carried twelve points cupped on the tops, but antler length was short. I reached for the movie camera and watched him go. The deer ran for miles, way along the range or weaving down to the bush far beneath. These were frightened deer, terrified of the brief glimpse one or two had caught of me. It was disappointing and unexpected.

I spent a cold, interesting day out on those Whitewater tops, glassing every peak for miles, watching, exploring, photographing. Isolated by cliff and chasm, they must be some of the most remote peaks in Fiordland, seldom penetrated on foot and the timidity of the main herds of deer was hard to explain, except for one dark thought. Poaching venison hunters slaughtering from their helicopters? Perhaps I'm wrong, but deer aren't wild without some good reason. No known party, either trophy or culling, had previously visited here in twenty years.

Russell and Wilby had had a tough unproductive day, for they didn't see any game down in the bush.

The weather was still threatening rain next morning as the three of us climbed to stalk the snowgrass tops. We sighted a medium-sized wapiti bull and several cows, but they disappeared into the mist near Expedition Peak. A red stag roared a challenge down the spur toward Madman's Creek. For a moment a breeze rolled the clouds back and we spotted him on a rocky point so down we hurried. But the breeze played tricks on us next time and whipped the mist aside while we were on an exposed snowgrass bench. The small stag, carrying only nine or ten points, whirled and fled.

Steady, insistent rain set in so we turned back for camp and were settled in the tent again by 10 am. All that day and the next it rained, but with a new fly covering the tent, and a little gas stove to cook on, we were warm and comfortable. Wilby cleaned the jet on the primus, but cooking was still slow. Wekas, three of them in fact, lived around our camp and seemed to enjoy the rain. One black one had an eye for bright objects such as my fork, but another brown bird loved venison. Standing in the rain inside the door of the tent, it wasn't content with scraps, but strolled in calmly and scooped up a whole slice of venison steak from the pan. I reached out with my bowie knife and tapped it gently on the head until it indignantly dropped the meat. One night Wilby grabbed a weka in his arms as it came out of the tent. It didn't struggle and when he put it down, just shook its feathers like an old hen, and reached calmly for another morsel. Keas were plentiful; two perched on our tent and pole while we were in the shelter. I like those cheerful, colourful mountain parrots, but they don't ever sleep. They would swoop screeching on to the guy ropes in the dark of midnight and wake us with their chatter. We cooked and yarned the time away, or played poker with a pack of miniature cards. Occasionally a distant bugle or roar would sound out of the swirling rain clouds to brighten our day.

The sixth day out from base camp dawned clear, and we were away early, out on to the high tops. Bands of fog shrouded the fiords, drifting and receding up the valleys. We skirted the now familiar Expedition Peak and eased over the ridge. A bull bugled ahead on a snowgrass hollow, but as we closed in we startled a sleeping red stag which bounded toward the wapiti herd. That spoilt our photographic opportunities, for the little band of five or six wapiti streamed off round the range. The elk only carried seven points, probably the same bull glimpsed nearby on Expedition Peak in the fog two or three days before.

Those deer ran for miles too, way along the divide, then crossed down into a tributary of the Whitewater. Hours later we glanced down there and saw the same young bull and his harem far below, on the bush edge. The bull soon spied our tiny forms a mile above, and immediately gathered his herd again and darted into the thickets.

Those wapiti were extremely timid, but we found one lovely red stag in the next snowgrass face. He came wandering up from the Whitewater bush gorge, bugling splendidly, pausing occasionally to mock-fight a tussock bush. The stag drank at a tarn, watched his reflection a moment, then playfully lunged his antlers into the water. He carried only eleven fine sweeping points, so we laid aside our rifles and crept to meet him with the cameras. Hearts thumping with excitement we stalked gradually closer, down through the rich tall tussock. At forty yards the stag eyed me curiously where I crouched half-concealed, having been caught crossing an opening. Click, click, shutters and cameras snicking. The stag bugled handsomely again, glanced up at Russell and Wilby and then nibbled the snowgrass. I took a dozen colour slides, then hurriedly finished a 25-foot reel of movie and added a few photos in black and white film while the fine, sleek, dark-coated stag ignored us disdainfully.

After some ten minutes of wonderful picture-making, I attempted to creep even closer, and worked in to within twenty-five or thirty yards. But the stag became uneasy and wandered back down the spur. Quite elated with our experience, we climbed back up the steep slope. A couple of hundred yards below the stag settled himself by the tarn and lay staring at us curiously. This splendid stag looked purebred red in every respect, with very dark pelage and typical red deer antlers, yet he bugled clearly instead of roaring. Here's a thought. Do the reds and wapiti imitate each other? They certainly respond to each others' roars and bugles. I have a pet red stag known as Tiki and he will clearly imitate a deep Hereford bull or the high-pitched yodel of a calf. One season, after a course of male hormone pills, Tiki roared for seven months nonstop!

There is a pleasant saddle between the headwaters of Madman's Creek and a remote, untrodden tributary of the Whitewater. Beyond the saddle rears Spot Hill, where Wilby and his brother Ross had each shot their respective fourteen-point bulls in different years. With the powerful binoculars and a favourable light we spied several wapiti bulls skylined on Spot Hill, but they certainly weren't fourteen-pointers.

Near Madman's Saddle Russell discovered a very old and weathered little fifteen-point wapiti head, split in two halves. It was only about thirty-seven inches long.

Over the range to the north we were deeply interested in negotiating the broad saddle which lies under the northern shadow of Expedition Peak, hoping to cross it to Horror Peaks and make a descent from there to base camp. But the whole mountain is absolutely sheer along its northern wall—mile after mile of ragged knife-edge plunging to the trees below. Heavy cloud rolled in toward sundown and there was cold rain all night and next day. We packed up our meagre supplies and wet tents and strode into the storm, back along the range to Ethne Saddle and down Ethne Valley the way we had come. But instead of descending the cliff into Ethne Saddle, we carefully followed an old deer trail which wound down through the bluffs. I had missed it by only a yard or two on the way up!

There was a red deer hind bounding gracefully into the trees in the little Ethne clearing, and a lone pigeon winging overhead. Back at base, a friendly black fantail greeted us, flitting in and out of the tent.

The weather cleared next morning, so we hastily repacked our wet swags and set out for Saddle Hill at 11 am, up the familiar Ethne Stream again to the saddle then east up a sloping ledge through the bush. An old deer track was well defined but definitely hadn't been used by any deer at all for some years. Soft green moss, which takes years to mature, had clothed the track, and there wasn't one lone deer mark disfiguring the vegetation. A very odd fact, which showed that the little herd of deer in Ethne Stream were an isolated, hermit band and that there had been no deer movements in or out of the area for years. Vegetation normally favoured by deer, such as the broadleaf shrubs, were plentiful, and hadn't even been nibbled.

We made excellent time up the deer trail and a tumbling stream and were above the bushline of Saddle Hill in five hours from the seashore. It was a windy, exposed ridge and we trimmed out a hollow in the bushes to rig the tent. A stand of tough, wind-lashed manuka and stunted dead cedars made wood-gathering easy.

With Russell in camp you never need fear you will sleep in. He invariably woke us around 5 am, a couple of hours before dawn, so as usual we were on the trail at first light. Wilby and Russell climbed the snowgrass of Saddle Hill, right over the skyline, while I explored a mile below in the tussock and slab rock. Similar in terrain to Expedition Peak, the Saddle Hill country is very steep on the north, but slopes off on the southern face before bluffs plunge into the bush. I skirted along just above the cliffs, glassing the occasional intriguing clearings in the Still-water or the remote Twin Falls Valley beyond. Deer sign was negligible, no fresh deer prints, and even the succulent mountain ranunculus plants were flourishing unchecked.

It was an odd fact that though animals are very few indeed around Saddle Hill, I could without trouble spot deer in the Stillwater Valley way below and wapiti on the far-away Twin Falls Peaks. Fifteen years ago Jack Hall stalked Saddle Hill, shot a fine thirteen-point bull from the tiny band of wapiti residing there —and they still haven't multiplied. Judging by the well-marked and long-disused deer trails along to Marguerite Peaks and Ethne Saddle this wasn't always so.

Away round the southern basin of Saddle Hill my glasses caught the movement of a heavy stag. I watched for a while until I glimpsed my two cobbers on the skyline. I waved them notice and climbed warily up a depression.

"That stag is worth taking," excitedly announced Wilby. "I can see three points on each top."

It was to be Russell's shot, we decided, so Wilby and I both rummaged in our respective packs for a movie camera apiece. Down we crept through the snowgrass, taking advantage of every hollow and rock. At 100 yards range, perhaps less, we peeped over the last knoll and saw the great stag still grazing placidly. The whirr of the cameras instantly alerted him; he glanced our way and Russell's Stiga blasted a shot away. The stag plunged down across a watercourse and Russell's second and third shots rang out. Still the stag was on his feet, apparently unhurt. Russell fired again and chips splashed from rocks close in front of us.

"Hell!" cried Wilby in anguish. "You've missed him. Your rifle is shooting way off."

Wilby tossed aside his Bell and Howell movie, snatched his old .303 and downed the stag. So Wilby took the trophy instead of Russell. Thinking back we recalled the previous evening when, after searching about for a reasonable camp site, Russell had grabbed his rifle loosely by the sling in one hand, his heavy pack dragging in the other. One hobnailed boot fouled the shoulder strap of the sixty-pound pack and Russell took a nasty tumble, his 30.06 and tender scope sight clattering onto the rocks.

The animal was a tremendous beast—it took three of us to haul him. He carried a twelve-point head, cupped on each crown. Antler length was thirty-nine and a quarter inches one side, thirty-seven and five-eighths the other and spread just under thirty-five inches. The antler structure was more or less characteristic of red deer, with no throwback, though I doubt it was a purebred red judging by the huge carcass and hint of blond in the coat. Caching the meat, antlers, and headskin cape on a prominent rock, the three of us travelled east along the divide, spending a pleasant day glassing toward the headwaters of the Stillwater and Edith Valleys. We saw or heard few animals, and on our range there appeared to be virtually no resident deer. There was a nine-point red stag grazing in the sun down towards Lake Katherine. That strange animal was only shedding the velvet, shreds of tissue still hanging lifeless from the new white and pink bone structure. Two very young and naïve wapiti bulls watched us from high on Saddle Hill. Even they had disappeared when we climbed the hill again next morning so, as the weather was deteriorating quickly, rain squalls sweeping up the Stillwater from the sea, we swung the frame packs to our resentful shoulders and hurried down through the moss-hung bush toward base camp so far below.

Heavy rain and low cloud spoilt our rather desperate plans for one last stalk. Whenever the fog and rain swirled aside we would step on to the shore, and focus the glasses on Horror Peaks. There were those same four or five wapiti grazing 4,000 feet above, tempting us.

Among our gear was a large tractor tube, inflated and sewn with canvas to make a very stable primitive boat. The aircraft people had advised us to bring some type of inflatable craft in case our landing site wasn't negotiable close into shore.

One evening I rigged up my bait caster with nylon line and fancy three-hook lure. The fish were there—I could see them drifting in the calm water—but they weren't biting until I hung venison on the hook. One after another I hauled them ashore. My delighted cries brought Wilby and Russell out in the rain. They started with nylon line and finished with a heavy hank of thick white twine and a young shark hook on it. Those unsophisticated fish would attack anything, following the venison-baited hooks right up to our feet.

Within an hour or so we landed between forty and fifty edible fish. Fifteen or more were great blue cod; one must have weighed eight pounds. Russell caught one red cod and the other fish were of a short, plump, sweet variety. Half a dozen ugly, spiny fish with bulging eyes and gaping jaws we tossed back in, and all the small ones. As you will no doubt realise, I'm no sea fisherman—to tell the truth they were the first sea fish I have ever landed!

Next morning I spent an hour or so fishing from the rubber dinghy, using our largest billy as landing net. With the crayfish boat due next day, we stocked up with sea fish to carry back to our hosts at Mararoa.

Late in the afternoon the rain eased so I made one last stalk, paddling across George Sound in the little round boat. Floating lightly on the water, subject to whim of wave and wind, I figured that if the tide were really running out, I might be the first deer-stalker ever to sail to Australia in a tractor tube. Way offshore it was a strange feeling, paddling hard for ten minutes, the far shore no nearer and distant tent still receding.

There is a good strip of bush across the sound under Horror Peaks and large bulls or stags frequented the area. The trees had been rubbed recently, always high up, but I saw no deer tracks fresh since the rain. Later I learnt that fishermen had loosed a shot or two at a fine beast on the beach there just on darkness one evening not long before.

We saw no wekas at our seashore camp, though on several occasions we heard their peculiar drumming call. A pair of sedate black swans cruised along the bush edge, and when the tide was in, flounder would drift among the shallow rocks. Russell actually speared one by stalking it ferociously, knife in hand. Photographed unawares on movie, my bearded Waikato mate looked just like the original wild native hunting for food.

Fiordland bird life is entrancing. On the high tops I secured a fine movie of the lively little rock wrens and at base I followed the engaging friendly fantails both black and pied, with my camera. There was a bellbird or two about and a few tuis swishing by.

Pigeons, unfortunately, were very scarce. We saw one cheeky robin but the drier beech forests to the east suit these birds better. We were disappointed there were no blue mountain ducks in Ethne Stream, for I recalled several of them over the saddle in the Stillwater. We did actually discuss a camera trip into the neighbouring Stillwater block to look for blue mountain duck but discarded the idea; if we had met the wapiti stalkers hunting there, they might have viewed our intrusion with a jaundiced eye.

One unwelcome visitor to our camp was a sleek stoat, weaving along the shore. Our tent was a good one, but the last night ashore torrential rain strained the seams, and we had to rig plastic tarps inside to steer aside the deluge over our sleeping bags.

Wisps of grey fog drifted across the sound as the *Koromiko* came cruising out of the dawn to take us back to civilisation.

Food for the Long Trail

I'VE SEEN SOME GHASTLY BREWS hashed out in the ranges, often accompanied by an apologetic remark such as:

"I always say a hunter should be thankful for any food at all, especially if it's hot."

Don't you believe it! At home we eat three good meals a day, plus the odd brew of tea or coffee. Stalking, a chap climbs far longer hours, burns up more energy and yet some hunters try to tramp for days on an empty gut, full of enthusiasm and damn all else.

One of the worst messes I can recall was long ago, high in the Ruahine Ranges up in Howlett's Hut. With cobbers Ivan Edwards and Wilby Oliver I had been doing a New Year reconnaisance trip early in 1948 and returned to the whare to find a couple of acquaintances guiding a small party of scouts. One of them, genial Les Bayliss, had shot a spiker, quartered a leg into large cubes and was busy rolling the bloody chunks of meat into a sticky mess of mixed flour and water. He splashed the awful concoction into a billy of water and heated it over the smoky, wet, birch fire. The "dumplings" had scarcely boiled when Les pronounced the mess cooked and ladled it out. I'll never forget those poor kids trying to swallow that horrible brew of raw venison and starchy, uncooked flour. You won't hunt far or fast on that sort of food for long!

There is another fraternity who claim they need nothing but a slice of stale bread for a hurried breakfast, and that a battered cake of crumbled chocolate and a miserable packet of raisins will keep them going all day on the hill. That's not for me either!

Years ago I remember stepping into an ancient rabbiter's hut in the Ruahines at the headwaters of the Pohangina River. The Tin Hut, as it was known, was destroyed in the Moorcock's bush fire of 1946. The Coldstream gang from Dannevirke were in occupation. They had a huge pile of white bread stacked in one corner, nearly to the ceiling, and they told me they were in for a fortnight and lived exclusively on bread and tea.

A stalker tends to eat and follow the example of his earlier companions. I did much of my early hunting with Viv Severinsen, and his stock food was bread, venison stew and porridge, day in and out. I followed his pattern for years, but lately have hunted with a wide variety of mates, both here and overseas, and my tastes have changed a little.

I remember tough cowboy Lloyd Tillett from Wyoming. When I sorted a loaf or two of bread to pack on a ten-day trip above the Greenstone tops, Lloyd was disgusted.

"I'm not carrying that rubbish," he insisted. "All I need is a

Wilby Oliver gazes down the Stillwater Valley. Lake Marchant lies under the fog.

The Mightiest Stag in Fiordland. This outstanding sixteen-pointer red stag is a joint trophy as both stalkers fired simultaneously.

Joe's River deluge. Cascading waterfalls swell the flooded river during a storm.

A hidden pool, called Welcome Lake, high in the Fiordland forests.

pound of salt and a packet of chewing tobacco." Chewing tobacco being a bit scarce in New Zealand, my American friend ate cigars! Lloyd literally lived out of a frypan, whether at home or hunting; he ate well-salted steak for every meal.

In India during a three-month hunting shikar in the jungles during 1952, we lived on meat, rice, and chapattis. The meat was usually excellent, either black buck antelope or fine venison such as chital or barking deer. We had samba too, but it is a very coarse meat. Alas, the Indian cooks insisted on dunking the lovely venison in curry, spices, and peppers so hot that we groped blindly for the water bucket to quench the fire in our gullets. Chapattis are thin-rolled slices of coarse flour and water, cooked briefly on a skillet. Tough and unappetising, they were nourishing.

In Alaska I hunted with outfitter Johnny Luster. There were no frills in Johnny's pack string. One of Johnny's wealthy clients remarked to me that Johnny had a reputation for having his hunters "eat rough, sleep wet, but bring home that game". In that outfit you more or less lived on steak, either bear, moose, caribou or Dall ram, and Betty Crocker pancakes liberally smeared with sticky maple syrup from a gallon can. If you wanted lunch you stowed a steak or two and pancakes in your pocket during breakfast at dawn.

Over the last few years I've taken to carrying a small aluminium frypan in my pack. I'm just a carnivore, but I'll travel further and faster on steak than any other food. Say what you like, venison stew is not very palatable and it takes ages to cook decently. I always figure it takes three hours' cooking to tenderise venison straight off the beast, and three hours to wait, squatting over a smoky fire or crouching late over a primus in a pup tent, is a long time.

You don't need much fat or butter in the pan to cook steak—just a smear on the bottom to save the steak from sticking. It's more or less grilled really. You need about a panful of steak each per hunter for the evening meal, and another panful apiece cooked up the night before ready to be carried cold on the long trail next day. Let the chap who wants it carry raisins or chocolate or bread for lunch; I'll settle for cold steak.

Now don't get the idea I'm writing this chapter for anything but the long, tough trail where you backpack all the way. If you're hunting out of an accessible base camp, then various nourishing tinned and fresh foods are readily available. The same applies to an air drop—many of the supplies are tinned foods.

Bread isn't a good food on the long trek. It's bulky, heavy and if you have stood on it once or twice, or used it as a pillow, it loses its character. After two or three weeks bread goes mouldy, too. Incidentally plastic bags encourage bread mould more than anything. But nevertheless a loaf or two is handy for daylight meals, especially early in the trip.

During our Fiordland hunt into the Whitewater block, we packed lighter and ate better than ever before. I don't think our packs ever weighed over sixty pounds and that included spare change of clothing, tents, cooking gear, and three cameras for myself alone. The secret is those excellent dried vegetables.

For the evening meal we always had one packet of dried peas or beans and when they had cooked a few minutes, we stirred in a packet of potato powder in the same billy. A pinch of salt and butter, plus liberal steak or venison stew and you had the basis of a good meal. Dried onions for the stew are wonderful and there are numerous other vegetables available.

Rice as a sweet is sustaining and pleasant. A billy of rice needs a little sugar and either a handful of sultanas or dried apricots. A pound or so of each will last three men a week or more and really give the rice a lift. Stir in a little dried milk when the brew is cooked; it thickens and pleasantly flavours the rice.

At one time I carried dried apples but no longer favour them. They're too bulky; apricots are better for carrying.

I'm not too partial to porridge at any time but can see its uses on the hill. It's quick and hot and can be reasonably edible if I fail to shoot something. Even my youngsters won't swallow Dad's porridge. With porridge it helps if you remember the salt and it definitely needs a sprinkle of sugar and dried milk powder. The recipe on the packet is usually worth following.

Beverages on the trail. Most of us like tea, with or without milk and sugar. Unfortunately sugar is heavy and condensed milk sticky and altogether too weighty. I'll settle for black tea and a pinch of sugar, though dried milk isn't very heavy. A change to instant coffee or Ovaltine can be very welcome and relatively weightless.

Soup is excellent on the trail, even as a midday break. Remember I mentioned that crumbled-up mouldy bread. Well after a fortnight or so you can toss all the crushed remnants and crusts in the billy with the soup—it makes a hot, palatable meal. If the butter is about gone and the jam and honey finished, soup is the best way of using up bread.

Hot scones are no trouble to make. Russell Sattrup likes dabbling with some self-raising flour. Mix up a batch with a little dried milk, water, salt (and maybe a sultana or two) to a dough and toss in the frypan until they start smoking. Then frizzle on the other side and serve hot.

I like to carry a few sweets and biscuits to have as a quick snack during the early day or two. Once I have meat then I'll gnaw a cold steak, but of course others may prefer their raisins.

Well, there it is. You hunt with me and you'll eat well and reasonably often and come back from a week's trip much fitter than you started. I've seen a lot of parties starve themselves with food so poor they couldn't eat it after three or four days. They become so exhausted they had to think up an excuse to abandon the hunt.

By the way, almost anywhere in New Zealand on a long pack trip away from huts, a little mountain stove of some sort is very handy indeed. Rough weather usually strikes at some stage, and with a primus you can sit out a foot of snow or ten inches of rain quite comfortably, cooking in the tent and warming it too.

There are other good foods which I usually leave behind or find too troublesome. Eggs for instance. Nourishing and easily cooked, they don't carry well at all, as my experience in Southland demonstrated.

In country where meat is scarce, or you are trophy hunting and really reluctant to shoot venison, then those light freeze-dried meat packets are very good.

By the way, there's nothing to cooking up a venison stew. Don't use your best cuts for stew. The back steak all goes into steak, and so do the best slices off the hind leg. Steak out the meat in slices across the grain to start with, then cut it as small as possible—into inch cubes at the largest. If there is no handy smooth rock available to carve on, the butt of your mate's rifle will do quite well. Don't be shy, use the largest billy available and fill it three-quarters full of raw red meat, even if it is a gallon container. Stew takes so long to cook decently, you want to make at least two full meals out of a brew, and it warms up quite well.

When the stew first boils it is difficult to avoid it frothing over, even on a very slow fire. And in the next two or three hours, while the stew simmers, you will have to top it up every half-hour or so with a mug of water. Remember a decent spoon of salt and half a packet of dried onions. Pepper to taste helps too. So do some carrots and if you like, when the stew is cooked you can stir in dried peas or beans for a little while, even the potato powder if you want all the stew in one goulash. Remember that when you thicken a stew with flour or potato powder it will stick and burn badly when you reheat for another meal. Come to that, any odd food remnants at all can go in a stew. Rice, cooked or raw, twisted tough crusts of ancient bread, stray raisins gumming up your pack—toss the lot in! Around the base camp a generous dash of Worcester sauce does no harm, but you won't be carrying that on a long trail.

Perhaps a brief summary of the supplies Wilby Oliver, Russell Sattrup and I packed in on our wapiti trip might be of use. As soon as the base camp was established we delved through the mixed pile of scattered boxes, bags, clothing, cameras, guns, fishing rods and assorted junk, and heaped the supplies on a tarpaulin.

Our first foray was to be into rough unknown country west of Ethne Saddle, so we sorted food for a week's hunting plus some emergency rations in case of storm or flood.

6 loaves of bread between us
3 lb butter between us
3 lb rice, maybe a bit more
$1\frac{1}{2}$ packets porridge between us
Under 2 lb sugar (inadequate)
1 lb milk powder in a tin between us
$\frac{1}{2}$ lb or so of honey in screwtop aluminium container
Small tin jam for party
$\frac{1}{2}$ lb salt. Pepper. Small quantity Ovaltine, instant coffee
$\frac{1}{4}$ lb tea
12 packets soup powder (Russell's favourite fodder)
1 lb sultanas between us
2 lb dried apricots for the party
Packet sweets and packet barley sugar
6 or 8 packets chocolate wheaten biscuits, mainly for a snack on the trail

6 packets assorted dried peas or beans
6 packets potato powder, plus a few packets of vegetables extra for emergency
1 lb or so of fat to cook the steak, and three or four lb of self-raising flour for scones

This was about the lot. As it was the trophy hunting period in Fiordland, no meat was available until late the third day out on the tops. Perhaps we carried a little extra rice and porridge than I've listed, but though the remaining food was more or less consumed I recall we had ample emergency salt, porridge, freeze-dried vegetables and rice to carry down off the range.

I haven't really figured it out, but the above supplies, split three ways, don't weigh up too badly.

A young New Plymouth stalker wrote to me and told an interesting tale of shooting his first deer up the Mokai. He mentioned the trouble he had carving it up for venison.

The two back steaks are the most easily available and the best meat on any deer. They lie in a long strip on either side of the backbone. If you haven't already removed the whole hide, slice off a strip of skin a foot or more wide right down the shoulders to the hips. That exposes the meat. Slip a knife down alongside the vertebrae and make a long cut close to the bone right down the backbone, with rib-bone or vertebrae projections stopping the depth of your cut. Then lay the blade flat on the rib or vertebrae and carefully slice off the back steak so it eases off in one long triangular strip, maybe two or three feet long. Slice across the grain into steaks about half or three-quarters of an inch thick.

Front shoulder meat is easily cut off but is best used for stew. There is too much sinew and a smallish eye of meat for a decent steak. To trim off the front leg, roll the beast over on to its back and from the brisket hack down along the ribs. The whole front leg will fall off, invariably in a pool of mixed blood, mud and birch leaves. Don't worry—that's where the minerals and vitamins come from!

The back leg or haunch provides more and better chewing. Roll the stag well on his side or back and slice fairly carefully along the groin. Too deep in the gut and you'll soon know it, as a gooey mess oozes out. Keeping the knife in good red meat, cut down toward the hips and you'll find a round socket bone. Ease the knife around that and the whole leg is yours. Have you got the pan on yet? Well, what are you waiting for?

The Mightiest Stag in Fiordland

I SWUNG UP the binoculars and gasped. "There's a tremendous stag up there. Could have a spread of forty-five inches."

Wilby focussed the 10 x 50's. "He's carrying a whole birch tree for antlers. Must have seventeen—eighteen points by the bunches on top."

It's those rare, brief moments of wonder that send the stalker slogging back into the farthest mountains.

Wilby Oliver and I had left home a week or so earlier in the landrover, crossed the ferry to Christchurch and driven from there to Milford in one long day. The people at Milford—whether managing the tourist hotel, handling a fishing craft, cooking at Johnson's Hostel or working the Milford Track—were all a helpful lot and we soon had unofficial transport arranged for journeying up the Milford Track to our stalking block.

Darky Thomas runs the Milford end of the track, and by 10.30 am next morning we were crossing the sound to Sandfly Point. Last year we had met Darky on the Clinton end of the track but now, minus his huge black beard, he was operating the jetboat on Lake Ada. It's a tough track on vehicles, and Darky's trailer was somewhat bent, down to one last stripped bolt. Wilby, Darky and I managed to tip the steel trailer completely over and with an axe, belt it back to fit new nuts and bolts.

We travelled by tractor and trailer up to Lake Ada, then enjoyed being guests of Darky and his jetboat up the lake. At the boatshed we heaved on our packs. Dave, a cheerful young Aussie working on the track, soon caught us up and yarned awhile. As we tramped up the well-known tourist walk, some three miles up the Arthur Valley from Lake Ada we came to a hanging valley which plunged down to add its waters to the Arthur.

There is a certain amount of doubt about the name of this

valley. The maps say Diamond Creek, but Milford Track guides and earlier hunters and explorers always refer to the area as Green Valley because of its striking evergreen parks of trees when viewed from distant McKinnon Pass.

My mate and I waded the Arthur River, had a quick meal and then cached quite a pile of food, fuel, films—even some ammunition. Dumpling Hill reared across the entrance to Green Valley, quite a formidable barrier. Nelson stalker Don Cummings and his party had pioneered a tough journey up and over the northern saddle of Dumpling years before. It looked steep—all waterfalls and rocky bluffs.

Wilby and I explored up the gorge south of Dumpling Hill. For a mile the going was good, open bush with even some deer sign. But soon we were in a nasty bush gorge, deep and damp, full of boulders and ancient windfalls. We swung down loose lawyer vines to cross, but deep swirling rapids tumbled down through the defile.

Somehow we scrambled up the gorge and eventually waded across, but the sodden bush on the other side was no better. There was no sign of either man or beast anywhere.

"It's getting dark," I stated. "We'll just have to camp somewhere."

On a damp slope we grubbed aside a few fern bushes, then by torchlight Wilby gathered wet fern for bedding while I strung up tent and fly.

Next day was 25 March and we were away early on up the gorge. We soon broke out to a lovely clearing ringed with birch bush and massive cliffs. An elevated fringe of black birches just north of the stream promised a likely campsite so we tramped across and dumped our packs. As I knelt by the rucksack a lone stag roared strongly way up the valley.

"Whose stalk?"

"Yours," said Wilby.

The Green Valley clearing was quite extensive, a beautiful park of long, marshy grass and vast areas of green ribbonwood. Keeping close to bush or bands of koromiko scrub, we hunted carefully, but the stag stopped roaring before we were halfway there. The stream meandered backwards and forwards and soon we had to wade its icy waters. There was heavy hoar frost on the grass. Crossing a sandy beach littered with flood debris I spotted a hind through the twisted legs of a sparse stand of lacebark. She was unaware of danger, twitching her ears casually at the sand-flies. Bent low, Wilby and I edged back across the stream and crept through waist-high niggerheads and scattered ribbonwood.

A hind went bounding across, followed by a bouncing fawn. I roared and the fleeing stag wheeled to glance back, then rushed after his hinds. I dashed up a faint deer lead through the low trees and roared again. The stag was 100 yards away on the edge of the next belt of ribbonwood. He halted abruptly, long top tines white-tipped. I flung up the 30.06 but the cold air had partly frosted the lens. The optics were too dim to count points, and, anyway, there was no time.

The post sight slid a third of the way up the broad dark shoulder and I touched off a bullet. I heard the sharp crack as the bullet hit, but the stag leapt away into the trees.

"You hit him all right, Keith. He won't go far."

We searched up the open grass leads, and swung through the trees, but still there was no sign, so after further searching we hunted for the spot where the stag had stood. I soon found a sign or two of blood on the frosted blades of coarse swamp grass. A chain ahead I found another, and circling wide ahead another grizzly crimson splatter.

"I can smell stag," muttered Wilby.

"Here he is!" I cried. Antlers showed above the koromiko bushes.

He was a tremendous beast, but the antlers were poor—only a nine-point head and one of the bays was oddly deformed. Shivering in the deep-shaded canyon and biting frost we trimmed off the fat, tender back steaks. Wilby hefted a back leg, found he couldn't carry it one-handed and had to stagger out with the weighty haunch cradled in both arms.

Leaving the venison to cool by the water we climbed through birch forest, criss-crossing a pleasant stream. A dry wash took us rapidly up the moraine above bush-level, so we took cover under a large boulder to glass the cliffs.

One lone hind high under the cirque of cliffs was all we could see. It was a sunny vantage spot, so we stayed a couple of hours, photographing, boiling the primus, glassing, yarning. Wet clothes, drenched in damp forest and frosted grass, were hung across the rock to dry.

A couple of keas came to call and one lone pigeon floated into a handy tree, but by the time I looked up after fitting the telephoto lens, it had gone.

About noon my mate and I wandered back down Green Valley, set up camp, then cooked a handsome meal of venison steak plus freeze-dried peas and Deb potatoes. Toward evening Wilby stalked the flats while I explored the bush towards Dumpling Hill to find a better route out.

At dawn next day cloud was gradually closing in. We stalked the ribbonwood flats early, but saw or heard no sign of deer. In fact not a deer had left a hoof mark anywhere in the valley since early the previous day. Only half a dozen deer now lived in Green Valley, but there had been more a few years earlier. Deer trails, once freely used, had grassed over.

I was carrying two Asahi Pentax cameras, plus spare closeup and telephoto lenses which interchanged between both instruments.

A plaintive blue mountain duck let me stalk close enough for a photo on black and white film, but by the time the telelens had been transferred to the other Asahi and its colour film, the duck was bobbing lightly down a riffle.

Our camp was dismantled and packed by 9.30 am. We climbed high into the bush, then angled down across to the lofty swamp saddle north of Dumpling Hill. A cascading waterfall bounded into the Arthur Valley below, so to avoid it we sidled down across Dumpling Hill. As we slithered down the steep damp face Wilby grabbed a loose vine and let himself down and out.

Down we went through the sparse birches, with never a sign of deer. We recoiled as an awful precipice yawned below, 1,000 feet of overhanging rock with the tops of the trees waving far below. Having reconnoitred left and right without success we crawled back up Dumpling Hill, heaving and panting, dragging ourselves and heavy packs up again by fern and tree roots. I made a further survey before climbing wearily again. Wilby cached his pack and disappeared for a long time.

Returning he rolled a careful smoke, scratched a match, and said quietly: "I think we can make it. It's pretty steep but the drop below is only about fifty feet. There is a bit of fern to swing across on and a small tree to grab beyond."

Wilby scrambled across, crawled down a bluff from one stunted tree to another, and leapt a gulch. Swinging off his pack he carefully strapped it to a sapling, then came back up the cliff. I handed first one rifle, then the other across, and followed in order to cradle both weapons again while Wilby climbed down a tree, then lowered the firearms gently. Down we went, from tree to tree, until finally we found a trace of deer, then a faint lead winding down and past the bluffs. Where the moraine spilled out at the base of Dumpling, we thankfully tossed aside our packs and supped spring water and cold venison steak.

At the mouth of Green (or was it Diamond?) Creek, we retrieved our cached supplies, waded the Arthur, and set off up the Milford Track. Four friendly Aussie girls, toting their packs, came striding down the track. They were "Freedom Walkers", they explained, heading down to camp at Diamond Creek Hut.

We yarned and stayed awhile at Quintin Hut, gratefully accepting a cup of tea. Bill Hewitt, manager of Quintin, had been up Staircase Gully recently, and had only seen a hind or two. Dave, the Aussie track guide, was just back from a quick stalk in the headwaters of the Clinton. He reported that deer were plentiful just over McKinnon Pass in the Clinton watershed, and were roaring well.

Supplies for Quintin Hut are now brought in by a helicopter, which also drops off a shooter in the surrounding valleys. Only five days before the "chopper" had slaughtered four stags on the ice right below the Sutherland Falls. At Milford we had been informed that the 'copter had recovered a total of eleven deer from the Arthur watershed during its latest foray, that they were the heaviest animals they had ever recovered, and also the best heads shot in the whole 1969 season. Of course just how big the heads were I don't know.

"All twelves and fourteens," one informant stated.

Another chap, Arthur Johnson, thought the best was an eleven.

Somehow antlers grow more points after they are shot. Way down the Arthur the previous year we had heard stories of Bill Hewitt's prowess: "A big twelve from Diamond Creek and a twelve and fourteen from the horse paddock at Quintin," we were told.

When asked, Bill Hewitt grinned. "The 'twelve' from Diamond Creek is that small ten over the Trackmen's Hut. I've never heard of a fourteen shot in the Arthur, but I did get a nice twelve and a ten-pointer one night in the horse paddock."

Late in the evening my mate and I trudged on up the track toward the majestic Sutherland Falls, crossed the Arthur River and plunged into the damp, heavy bush. It was raining gently as we pitched camp.

Steady rain was still falling next morning as we packed and climbed Staircase Gully. For a while the travelling was good, but we scrambled up the gorge in the usual tangle of rotting logs, moraine, and moss.

Above the rapids there was a small, delightful clearing, placid and pretty. Ribbonwoods were in full bloom, their fallen white blossoms literally carpeting the ground. We saw no deer or animals, only a pair of agitated blue mountain ducks being pestered by a bunch of keas. Waterfalls were showering down the surrounding cliffs and it looked as if we were in for some real Fiordland rain. We hunted for a campsite safe from flooding, and settled on a gravel shoulder sheltered in the ribbonwoods.

Cutting a great pile of dripping fern, we piled it into the tent, and covered it with a sheet of plastic. By 2.30 pm we had the camp set up, so dragged off our wet clothes and crawled in. We were appalled to find the green tent fly was leaking badly, and the pup tent too, in spite of recent "proofing". Mind you, the tent wasn't exactly new. Wilby and I had carried that same tent up the Stillwater River in 1952, and this was 1969.

Drip! Drip! Drip! Wilby caught my glance. For twenty years he had been rolling his sleeping poke in an oiled black japara cover. "I know. I know," he muttered. "You're going to sacrifice my good cover." We sliced it open. I then shed every shred of clothing and pranced naked in the Fiordland downpour to drape the japara over the tent.

It turned nearly all the rain aside, though some still come under, creeping along the ridge pole.

The rain teemed down all night and next day. We lay in the tent, played crib and cooked the last venison steak from Green Valley. By 3.30 pm we were both tired of the cramped tent so shed our dry clothes, dragged on the wet ones and headed into the rain to stalk the valley. First down the ribbonwood flats, then upstream where we noted a geologist's old campsite high on a cold, birch spur surrounded by swamp. Yards of heavy plastic sheeting had been abandoned and with our leaking tent in mind, we dragged the plastic clear. But keas or wekas had holed it in dozens of places.

There was heavy birch forest toward the head of Staircase Gully and old deer trails criss-crossed it in profusion. But there was no fresh deer sign. Towards dark the rain eased and clouds started to break. Cheered by the prospect of a fine day ahead we planned a trip toward the Light River Saddle.

But soon after dark steady rain set in again. There were three or four inches of rain during the night and, judging by the billy, approximately an inch of rain per hour all next day. Torrents of water poured out of the swirling rain clouds high above. Waterfalls cascaded everywhere, dozens in sight from the tent-door. "The only things roaring in these valleys are the waterfalls," Wilby remarked.

A lone weka visited our tent occasionally, but it was a careful and suspicious creature. The bird was attracted by plastic bags, and would sneak up, grab one, and rush off in glee.

About 4.10 pm the rain was lighter, so I donned wet clothes and invited Wilby to accompany me up the valley. He declined, figuring that it was hopeless. I tramped fast up through the dripping birches and flowering, fragrant ribbonwood groves.

At the upper bush level, Staircase Gully narrows and angles sharp right up a defile to the north. A well-defined game trail, quite devoid of any fresh deer sign, climbed steeply towards the cramped pass half a mile above the bush. Mist and cloud swirled low above the pass, but for a brief moment the rain eased enough to spy three or four deer etched starkly against the skyline 1,500 feet above. Staircase Stream is still a formidable torrent right to the pass where it gushes out from under the moraine.

Cupped in the valley, ringed by fearful mountains rich with glacial ice, is a tear-drop lake half a mile long. I climbed above the pass to survey the hidden basin, then glanced up into the clouds to see a big stag climbing slowly, silhouetted on a jagged spine. I grabbed for the rifle but before I could snatch the rubber scope-cover aside, the clouds billowed down.

The stag carried quite a large head, well-shaped. Five minutes' hard looking for deer, then I turned back for camp, hurrying down through the sombre and shadowed forest to beat the dusk.

After three days of incessant rain, there were stars in the sky on the morning of 30 March. We were up early, breakfasted and were away by the fading starlight. Bands of dense mist skirted each peak but the rain had gone.

A stag roared strongly, the first roar we had heard in Staircase Gully. From camp he sounded a scant half-mile up the valley, so we proceeded cautiously. But soon we realised the beast was far above, high on the precipitous range north of Staircase Canyon. Climbing through the sodden upper bush, I suddenly halted and handed my rifle to Wilby.

"What's the matter?" he asked.

"These mountains are so high above a man has to tilt his head right back to see the top. I'm sick of hair falling in my eyes." Reaching for the sheath knife I hacked off generous chunks of damp hair. "Now I'll be able to see to shoot a stag."

We climbed rapidly to the pass and soon spied a large lone stag walking purposefully away from us, climbing the bluff trail west of Staircase Lake. Below the rugged cliffs, down near the lake, a little herd of five deer could be seen. There were two hinds and their fawns wandering about grazing, while the stag, a very dark animal, lay watching. From the bluffs above, the deer were still a long 350 or 400 yards below, but the stag didn't in any case appear a likely prospect, perhaps a small twelve-pointer.

The Staircase Gully-Light River Saddle is a rather wide area of pleasant tarns and snowgrass hummocks, but the Light River Valley beyond looked a cold, bush-clad chasm. There was a sunny face south of the pass and high above a steep, precipitous slope quite a large herd of deer grazed or sunned themselves.

I swung up the binoculars and there was the huge stag.

As I had shot the last stag, the nine-pointer in Green Valley, it was Wilby's first chance. I suggested we shoot from where we were, but Wilby declined—the range was too long. He figured to scale the cliff, climb high, and cross over down on to the deer.

But we hadn't gone 100 yards when a strong breeze wafted up from Staircase Gully, taking our scent directly towards the deer. Three of the closest animals were immediately alarmed. A small six- or eight-point stag wheeled and pranced. Two hinds joined him, hooting nervously.

"Come on. Let's get back and shoot before they all run."

Crouching low, we scuttled back down through the heavy rocks. The angle was so high above that we had to stand behind a huge boulder and tilt our rifles skyward.

"Keith, if I can't hit him, you be in too!"

That stag looked a long way off now. I fished in my hip pocket and carefully pushed an extra shell into the breech to supplement my meagre four-shot magazine. Though three or four deer were still performing nervously, the stag, much further away, now lay down behind a rock; only his head and antlers were visible with binoculars.

When Wilby was ready, with left wrist comfortably snuggled on his rolled parka, I cupped my hands and roared hard at the mountain monarch. The stag remained there, but put his head back and answered. I roared again, my loudest effort, and the stag climbed unhurriedly to his feet and glanced our way.

"This is it. Here goes!" whispered Wilby.

His .303 rang out, but the bullet missed.

Then I fired, and Wilby shot again.

"You're away low and to the right," I exclaimed as I saw stone chips fly from Wilby's second shot.

My second bullet was another miss, so I angled the 30.06 rifle way above, aiming level with the top of the stag's high antlers.

Both rifles went off absolutely simultaneously and the stag collapsed, pitching down the snowgrass slope.

"Aw . . . Stop! Stop!" prayed Wilby, aghast. Another foot and the stag would have plunged 2,000 feet down the cliff.

A deer trail angled up the cliff and we climbed rapidly, eager to inspect our trophy. But even so, it took twenty-five minutes to reach him. When still two or three hundred yards away, two likely stags came over the skyline from the Light River Divide, and trotted up past our kill. We watched them go.

The stag was magnificent. Great massive antlers curled in and way back, heavy with points. The left antler—a remarkable $43\frac{3}{8}$ inches in length—carried nine good tines. The right antler sprouted seven points but the tops on this side had been badly mauled in a fairly recent fall, probably late in velvet. Several points were blunted and considerably shortened where they had been broken off, but all brow bay and trey tines on both sides were excellent. The broken-topped right side is still $40\frac{3}{8}$ inches long, with spread $35\frac{1}{2}$ inches, certainly not the 45-inch width I had guessed at from way, way below. Not a particularly large animal, the beast was coated dark red, and appeared to be of pure red deer origin.

The kill was a joint effort. We had both shot together and both bullets were vital hits—one was square in the base of the neck, and the other projectile pierced the shoulder dead-centre. The range was tremendous. Figure it out for yourself.

I handle a scope-sighted 30.06, fire 150-grain silver-tip bullets sighted dead in at a little over 200 yards. Both bullets had hit the centre of the body. Take a foot to the top of his back, another to the level of his skull, plus three feet to the top of his antlers. That gives a bullet drop of five feet or more.

Over three days of continuous torrential rain hadn't done our cameras any good. In spite of loving care they had drawn moisture, which condensed inside the lens immediately the warm sun struck them.

Leaving the instruments perched on a rock to thaw out, we climbed a few yards to the Light River Divide. We must have been up nearly 6,000 feet and there seemed as much empty space below on each side. To the south our jagged spur towered above Staircase Gully to hide Lake Quill and the Sutherland Falls. On the western side an expansive tussock face sloped towards the Light River, then plunged off a high cliff to the bush somewhere far below. North reared an impressive array of ragged spines, known vaguely on the maps as "Terror Peaks".

Photos recorded, we trimmed off the headskin, antlers, and meat. Wilby dropped the venison and headskin into his capacious frame pack, while I strapped the massive antlers on to my little stalking pack.

"We could take the stag's liver too," suggested my cobber. "There is only one spoonful of porridge and half a mug of rice left in camp. I'll never forget the first time you served half-raw liver! It was years ago in the Urewera, and I remember you saying, 'Liver wants cooking in the dark and eating in the dark and so long as it's warm it's cooked.' "

Getting down the cliff with the trophy was quite unpleasant. I had to sidle with my face to the rock as the wide antlers either side overbalanced me badly. Wilby paused to take a movie of my efforts, but I was too busy feeling for a toehold fully to appreciate being a film star.

On a snowgrass ledge I stepped a little more easily and promptly slipped. The blunt right antler ripped my trousers through and gouged a nasty gash right across one thigh.

"Just as well that antler was broken. A sharp tine would have gone right through your leg," observed Wilby.

It would have too. Even so, I'd have a bruise scar to show for months yet.

Down in the Staircase-Light Saddle three carefree keas came to visit. As always, we photographed them, then Wilby's hand sneaked out and clutched one. Objecting violently, the kea sank a ferocious beak into his index finger. While Wilby held the protesting kea, I plucked out a few of those pretty orange feathers from under the wings. We figured they would make likely trout lures. When released the bird just hopped on to a nearby rock, ruffled up its feathers, then came hopping close to say hello again.

Swinging the trophy across my shoulders, we descended into Staircase Gully, down off those stupendous peaks, carrying the antlers from the mightiest stag in Fiordland!

The Trail to Never Never

A THOUSAND FEET below a lovely stretch of still, dark water brooded in the morning sunlight. The lost lake called Never Never was in sight at last, well hidden in a remote canyon of the Harrison River.

I wonder who's heard of Lake Never Never or even the Harrison River? I know Fiordland fairly extensively but had to search a large-scale map to locate either place. Bill Axbey, Conservator of Wildlife at Queenstown, is the Government chap who spends his life looking for kakapo and other rare birds in Fiordland. He wrote:

"One other place I can suggest for a good red head and a chamois is the head of the Harrison. I think that country could carry a record chamois head provided numbers haven't got too high. An odd deer had moved in from John O'Groats about eight years ago and the head basin should carry something good by now. It's relatively untouched and the Kaipo country just north produces good timber."

My mate Wilby was immediately enthusiastic. "I can do with a decent chamois," he stated with conviction.

"All right, Wilby, you take every buck chamois we see, and I'll just carry out the big fourteens and sixteens," I replied.

"It's a deal!"

Whether there is game ahead or not, there is a powerful magnet in new country, far places where man has seldom trod.

The Harrison River is a lonely canyon winding into the stupendous mountains north of Milford Sound. Mists wreathed Mitre Peak and Mt Pembroke as a month later we approached Harrison Cove in the crayfish boat *Sea Gold*. Des Carter, the genial skipper, ticked off the almanac. "I'll be back Monday or Tuesday of next week," he said. "But if anything goes wrong, light a smoke smudge or do a haka on the beach. Someone will see it!"

He waved us ashore and Wilby and I set about seeking a base campsite. On the extreme tip of the bush point by the Harrison River, someone, probably trout fishermen, had camped, but the place didn't appeal. For one thing a high tide had recently washed right through the deserted camp. Further in the bush we found another old site, possibly used by Bill Axbey eight years before. It was level, dry, and reasonably close to the Harrison for water.

"No old rotten trees leaning over the tent either," I remarked.

We strung up Wilby's brand new orange nylon tent, a capacious 9 x 7, five feet high. A fly was stretched above. That afternoon we spent fleshing and salting the headskin of our Staircase Gully trophy and cleaning the skull. For lunch I fried a large brown trout, a present from three Americans and Canadians fishing Lake Ada. Another of their trout did for tea.

Towards nightfall we gathered some of the tough segments of meat jettisoned from the stag skull, and tried them as fish bait. Wilby, with a hand line, soon had ten good fish, butterfish and blue cod, wriggling on the rocks, but I found my son Lex's bait-caster rod had a broken tip. The only fish it landed was foul-hooked!

Recalling that Anita Bay, further down Milford Sound, is famous for greenstone, I did considerable searching in the receding tide, but found only a couple of low grade samples of nephrite.

Light rain swept in to dampen our fishing, but the weather was pleasantly cloudy as we set out early next day. The first few miles upstream were fairly easy travelling. The bush was quite open, with little undergrowth, odd considering that no deer or game had ever browsed the valley. A faint trail was occasionally discernible close to the river, and its presence was quite definite where some creature had hopped down, across, and past a shallow side-stream. Not an animal trail, but probably a bird track we thought, wondering about kakapo.

Past Pembroke Creek the Harrison becomes shallow, turning a couple of sharp angles before disappearing into a narrow canyon. The wide crossing, boulder-studded, looked shallow, but soon we were well above our knees in fast water, with a surging channel ahead.

"Wait here. I'm going back for a pole."

Pitching pack, cameras, and rifle atop a boulder in midstream, I retreated and knifed a couple of stout saplings from a bushy little island.

Waist-deep and very swift, the Harrison could be dangerous unless in really low water. The gorge ahead seemed never to end. We crawled over huge, moss-encrusted boulders and rotting windfalls, while alongside the mighty river spewed down in endless rapids and foaming falls.

Three hours later we pushed through to a wide bush basin with a couple of pleasant streams pouring down from glaciers to the west. Still no sign of game or any other wildlife. A lone pigeon and a bellbird were the only birds noted.

Exploring the broad bush valley of the middle Harrison was no cinch either. Twenty to thirty years ago a gale had toppled acres of huge birches in a swamp and now they were disappearing under a vigorous regrowth. We crawled under the bulging giants, pushing packs ahead, or climbed laboriously over the sodden trunks and rotting branches.

"Haven't seen anything like a reasonable campsite since we left base," muttered Wilby.

I reached for the aerial map again. "Could be a spot near that island ahead."

The day we had left home, my wife had presented us with two aerial photos of the whole Harrison watershed. The large 30 x 30 we studied, then left behind, but a small 8 x 8 print was absolutely invaluable, portraying every bend in the river.

Moir's Guidebook gives a sketchy but reticent account of the Harrison, a tramping party having once crossed over the tops from John O'Groats. Perhaps other trampers had prowled the Harrison since, but no previous stalker was known to have reached the headwaters.

The packs were dragging heavily as towards dark we made camp in a shingle fan reasonably high above the river. A lone and plaintive blue mountain duck came to visit and stay as I fried the evening meal, tasty sea fish carried from Harrison Cove.

Stars could be seen in the sky at nightfall but it was raining steadily by daybreak. We pushed on up the left bank, climbing steeply through the sodden trees. By 11 am the rain was really teeming down, waterfalls spouting down the surrounding mountains. The aerial map showed Moulin Creek watershed and Lake Never Never not far ahead, so we made camp well back from the main stream and its rapidly rising flood. Few of the tent pegs would drive in the boulders, so most of the guy ropes were anchored with weighty stones. We strung up my ageing pup tent and fly, and slung a couple of pieces of plastic over the leaking tent for good measure. Plastic stops the rain all right, even in Fiordland, but by morning condensation inside the tent was very bad.

Lying atop a very thick bed of dripping fern with a sheet of plastic on top was quite comfortable, and we yarned the afternoon away, quaffing sweet billy tea. Boiling up of course was no problem with a tiny gas primus inside the shelter.

The rain came down in torrents for some five hours, then suddenly eased. We changed back into soaked clothing and went to reconnoitre the next day's route. The Harrison headwaters are normally quite shallow, but now we could barely cross the stream.

An hour and a half's scrambling up cliffs and through dense scrub found no easy trail ahead, though a huge bare rock way up the Moulin slope caught our attention. "Baldy" Rock made a good landmark above the trees, and we sketched out a possible route from camp to Moulin Creek.

Our third morning on the Never Never trail dawned bright and clear. Beyond Moulin Valley, which comes in from the west, the Harrison disappeared in a deep narrow gorge, birch-clad, tumbling down from Lake Never Never to the north. Clambering through and under boulders and dead falls, we wasted no time, but it still took two hours' persistent scrambling to reach the lake.

"We should be lower, way down by the outlet, instead of

perched 600 feet up here on a bush cliff," Wilby pointed out. "Then we can go round the beach on the lake edge."

But Lake Never Never had no beach. The cliffs plunged straight into the deep, dark, sombre depths.

Up we went again, out to a basin above the timberline. Birches gave way to a jungle of snow-flattened alpine scrub, twisted and tough. We literally crawled under, pushing the rifles ahead, struggling, panting, and cursing! Beyond the bluff we still had naïve visions of snowgrass ahead, or an easy slope. But the scrub shelved off to a frightening precipice plunging sheer into the lake. The intertwined leatherwood had been awful, but slick bare rock on edge for hundreds of feet was worse. Clutching the strong leatherwood branches, greasy with black moss, we dragged ourselves up from tree to tree, kicking wildly to gain a precarious foothold. Once my rifle slipped and caught Wilby squarely on the skull as he struggled too close below.

And never a sign that game had ever trod these hills. High above the bare rock cliff, Wilby took the lead. The precipice was quite perpendicular, the still, cold water far below, but gnarled scrub bushes clung to the mountain. We climbed across, swinging from one stunted growth to the next, weighing distances and judging the sturdiness of those slender twigs ahead. Our lives literally depended on their strength. Perhaps thirty, fifty feet below another bush would impede our fall but it wasn't a cheerful thought. Another angle not worth considering was the possibility of landslides. Great avalanches frequently sweep whole mountainsides bare. Would our sudden weight start a rockfall or merely wrench the whole tree from its tenuous hold on the cliffs?

But you don't think of that, ever. You must go on to meet your destiny, that eleven-inch buck chamois on the heights ahead, or fourteen-point stag.

Five hours from camp we finally smashed through to the shores of Never Never beyond the cliffs, and made our way down to a lovely basin rich in mountain flowers. All around reared tremendous peaks, heavy with blue glacier ice. A few ribbonwood trees, favourites of deer, skirted the head basin, and the leaves had been nibbled a little. Further on, we noted the fresh hoof marks of a chamois in the sand.

But we saw no game. The deer were long gone, months, perhaps even a year before, swinging lifeless carcasses under a helicopter. The snowgrass head basin, blocked by deep Lake Never Never and its encircling cliffs, would be a murder trap. We knew that at least one chamois still lingered but we saw him not.

Thought of the awful five-hour struggle back past Lake Never Never appalled us, so we explored a new route. High under the northern cliffs we wriggled up a rock chimney, out to a spine of snowgrass. A game trail, long unused, led out and up to the open tussock tops toward the John O'Groats Saddle. The rotting carcass of a large buck chamois warned us not to slip.

The John O'Groats Saddle proved to be a pleasant pass but we couldn't linger. We angled along an easy snowgrass slope to Lake Pukutahi, a pretty gem of water perched high up in the mountains. Its Maori name suggests that the ancient Maoris knew this route. Of deer we saw no sign whatever, but here and there we saw a few dried-out chamois droppings.

Beyond Pukutahi we dropped down through sparse tussock and grey, bare slab rock toward Moulin Creek's junction with the Harrison. Down in the tangled bush below the two streams joined and tumbled towards our camp. Turning slightly back into Moulin's watershed, a narrow spine of birches led precipitously down into the gorge. We clambered warily down the trunks and stunted bushes, making excellent time.

Once I was surprised to find the hoof marks of a chamois in the moss, so when we finally hit Moulin Creek we looked wearily up the valley. It seemed a likely place, with stunted bush opening out to a hanging valley ringed with cliffs.

Wilby handed out a last ration of chocolate.

"Come on. I know it's late, but this is Fiordland. Could be raining hard tomorrow and we would never know if there was a twelve-inch chamois up there waiting to be shot."

Slowly, tiredly we trudged up the shadowed chasm, dragging up over a rock ledge scrabbled bare by tiny chamois hooves. Brick-brown nipples of garnet studded a tough metamorphic rock, so while I fossicked about for samples, Wilby hunted on to the headwaters.

We could understand how the deer disappeared, but the complete absence of chamois from the entire headwaters was quite puzzling, especially as they had been much more widespread.

It was dusk as we weaved down through the swamp cypress

and tanekaha, aiming for Baldy Rock's prominent dome. Smooth, rounded, that huge boulder must have been 300 feet long and half as high.

That's the way to go. Up past Baldy Rock, across Moulin Creek then up the birch spur to the glacier-slick bluffs below Pukutahi Lake. Then along the tussock slopes and down the John O'Groat's game trail to Lake Never Never.

But as Wilby says: "Never, never, ever, will I hunt the Never Never Trail again!!"